Study Abroad and Immigration 101

Ashwin

Dedication

This book is dedicated to all its readers, encompassing students, parents, consultants, education providers, and prospective migrants who share the common aspiration of making the dream of moving abroad a reality. Whether you're seeking motivation to study overseas or pursuing immigration intentions, this dedication is for you.

I genuinely hope that the information contained within these pages serves as a guiding light on your journey, for there is nothing more fulfilling than the pursuit of making not only your life but also the lives of your loved ones truly beautiful.

Acknowledgment

I would like to dedicate this book to my mother, Jamna, and my father, Hasmukh, who have given me endless and selfless love. To my dear mom, a lovely lady filled with boundless love for her child, I dedicate my work to you and want you to know that your little boy has grown up. To my dad, a man brimming with wisdom, I hope to hear you say that you are proud of me.

To my wife, Meeta, thank you for always supporting my extra hours in business and loving me so well throughout all the phases of this hectic and wonderful life we share.

And to my pillars of strength: Drashti, Ankit, Vishwa, and our Chief Excel Officer, Aarav.

Table Of Contents

Dedication ii

Acknowledgment iii

About the Author vii

Preface viii

Getting Started: Why Study Abroad 1

How To Choose the Right Program 15

Finding the Right Funding Sources 23

Studying in the USA 31

-Studying in Canada 42

Studying in the UK 50

Studying in Australia 57

Studying in Singapore 65

Studying in Dubai, UAE 75

Studying in Denmark 83

Studying in the Netherlands 90

Studying in Sweden 97

Studying in Switzerland 103

Studying in the Russian Federation 109

Studying in Germany 114

Studying in Italy 122

Studying in Spain 131

Studying in France 140

Studying in Hungary 149

Studying in China 156

Studying in Ireland 163

Studying in New Zealand 168

Studying in Japan 176

Studying in India 185

Ensuring Your Safety Abroad 190

Immersing Yourself in the Host Culture 195

Making the Most of Your Time Abroad 199

Seeking Immigration While Studying Abroad 207

Studying Abroad Experience for Global Growth in Country of Birth 212

Wrapping It All Up! 215

About the Author

Ashwin is an executive coach with over 33 years of experience in helping individuals and organizations enhance their leadership skills and achieve their missions. He has worked with senior and junior-level directors, as well as CEOs, with the primary goal of enabling them to maximize their performance.

Throughout his career, Ashwin has counseled approximately 40,000 individuals, collaborating closely with them to unlock their true potential and optimize their effectiveness.

He has also held leadership roles in various companies, including notable organizations such as Real Value, Standard Chartered Bank, Citibank, Axis Bank, and more.

Preface

Welcome to the world of international education, a realm where students broaden their horizons, challenge their limits, and set forth on journeys that can be truly life-transforming. This book serves as your guiding light through this captivating adventure.

In an era defined by global connectivity and boundless opportunities, the idea of studying abroad has become a beacon of hope for countless individuals seeking not just an education but an experience that shapes their future. As you turn the pages of this book, you'll encounter the intricate details of international education.

From the bustling campuses of American universities to the serene classrooms of Japanese institutions, each chapter presents a checklist tailored to the unique experience of studying in a specific country.

Studying abroad is more than just earning a degree—it is an adventure in self-discovery, cultural appreciation, and personal growth. As you navigate these chapters, remember that this book is more than a resource; it is your trusted companion. It provides practical guidance and valuable insights to equip you with the knowledge and inspiration needed for this life-changing journey.

So, fasten your seatbelt, open your mind, and prepare to explore the world through education. Your journey begins here, promising to be one of the most exciting and transformative experiences of your life.

Chapter 1

Getting Started: Why Study Abroad

Gaining Access to knowledge or studying, in general, has been around for as long as one can remember. Studying or learning is perhaps as old as time in several cases. However, have you ever wondered how the concept of studying abroad or international education came to be in the first place?

The traces of international studies can take us as far back as 1190 CE when Emo of Friesland decided to travel from the Netherlands to study at Oxford University in England. This started a pavement for international exchange in Europe for the next 800 years.

Ever since the adventure that Emo of Fricsland took, the concept of studying abroad has become a lot more common than one might think. Almost every college student dreams of getting a higher education from prestigious universities around the world. Not just that, foreign universities or foreign exchange programs, along with other facilities, help the students come and study in their institutes.

International education, or the idea of studying abroad, has become far more popular than one might expect and continues to grow rapidly. It is a trend that shows no signs of slowing down.

Of course, there was a time when COVID-19 disrupted many plans for international education. However, things are changing, and now may be one of the best times to pursue studying abroad.

The purpose of this book is simple: to help individuals navigate the process of studying abroad. As mentioned earlier, the concept of international education has existed for ages. However, more people are now embracing it—and for good reason. Despite its many benefits, one of the biggest challenges remains that many individuals feel overwhelmed or lost in the process.

The rut is that they are not sure about where to get started and what to do first. Surely, studying abroad is not as easy as getting admitted into your local college or university as there are several tests involved in the process that are mandatory for a student before they even begin.

This tedious process alone discourages countless students from pursuing their dreams of studying abroad, especially when they look at the laundry list of things they need to look after to have a 'chance' at their dream university. Yes, a chance. Not even a confirmed admission.

However, what if I tell you that the entirety of this process is a lot easier than you might have thought? You do not need to go through all the hoops, and you can study abroad. Don't worry; there is no shortcut being sold, but there are ways that you can make your dream of studying abroad a lot easier.

At <u>Moving Abroad: Study, Stay or Work – Your Ultimate Guide</u>, we offer a one-stop solution to help you achieve your dream of studying abroad in any country you wish to emigrate to. We take pride in providing an expert team and a comprehensive personality testing system designed for everyone.

Accessibility is key—it has become essential for everyone to gain valuable insights about themselves. To support this, we offer both online and face-to-face counseling, which includes aptitude and personality assessments.

Our goal is to ensure that students striving for admission to their dream universities or colleges have the best possible chance—without the burden of unnecessary obstacles.

As a business, our mission is simple: to make international education a reality for everyone.

Moving Abroad and Making Your Life Easy

It's safe to say that moving abroad can be a challenging process for many. However, we're here to make it easier for anyone planning to study, migrate, or work overseas.

How do we do that? By guiding you through every step—whether it's securing admission to a foreign university, navigating migration procedures, or finding opportunities to work abroad.

We've all experienced attending local schools and colleges, but for many, studying in another country is the most fascinating and transformative experience.

One of the greatest mantras to keep in mind during this journey is:

"You are not a tree."

No situation is permanent. If you find yourself unhappy with your new city, job, or school, or if you feel the place has nothing to offer, you have the power to change your circumstances. The worst thing you can do is believe you must simply "put up" with an unfavorable situation. You can explore new opportunities, relocate to a different place, or even move back home until you find the right fit.

Living abroad is a choice, not an obligation. There's no reason to make such a significant life change if it doesn't bring you happiness and fulfillment.

Make the most of your experience in a new city and return home with your head held high.

It's clear that moving abroad through the proper channels is only half the battle. The real challenge lies in finding the right program that aligns with your strengths and aspirations.

Fortunately, we're here to help you find the right path, ensuring that you make the most of your opportunities and do it the right way.

How Can One Migrate Abroad?

Moving abroad can seem like a daunting task, but there are several paths to make the process more manageable:

- **Work Visa Migration** – Securing a work visa, finding the right job opportunities, and advancing your career can be a great way to migrate.

- **Study-Based Migration** – Studying abroad is another excellent option for those looking to further their education while exploring new opportunities.

- **Permanent Residency (PR)** – Many individuals aim for permanent residency, and fortunately, countries like Australia and Canada, among others, offer PR visas to those who qualify. You can always check the latest eligibility criteria for different countries.

- **Investment & Entrepreneurship Migration** – Many developed and progressive nations encourage potential investors and entrepreneurs, making this another viable pathway to migration.

While the process can feel overwhelming, the right guidance can make all the difference. We're here to help you navigate every step, from understanding financial requirements and visa processes to making the necessary preparations for a smooth transition. With our support, moving to a different country and pursuing your dreams can become a reality.

Benefits of Studying Abroad

But why should you study abroad? This question has been at the forefront for many, and the answer comes with countless advantages.

The benefits of studying abroad are, of course, subjective. However, most people can easily understand and relate to them, as they often aspire to similar opportunities for themselves.

In the following sections, we will explore these advantages in detail, helping you see why studying abroad could be one of the best decisions you make.

The Exposure That Comes

Although studying abroad may not be for everyone, the exposure it offers is undeniable. One of the greatest benefits is the opportunity to explore the world and immerse yourself in different cultures.

Living in a new country allows you to experience diverse customs, traditions, and activities while discovering uncharted territories. While it may seem overwhelming at first, the more you explore and learn, the more comfortable and enriched you become in your new environment.

Another advantage is the ease of traveling to neighboring countries. For instance, if you study in France, you'll not only have the chance to explore different parts of Europe with minimal hassle but also visit nearby North African countries, broadening your global perspective even further.

Quality Education

This one should be a no-brainer for anyone considering studying abroad—quality education is a priority for most students. While local education systems offer great opportunities, studying abroad allows you to experience how different cultures approach learning.

You'll immerse yourself in an educational system that differs from what you're used to. Though it may be challenging at first, the exposure will push you to grow both academically and intellectually.

Additionally, studying abroad provides the chance to learn new languages and refine your skills. While English speakers may initially prefer to stick to their native language, over time, the ability to speak or at least understand multiple languages proves to be an invaluable asset.

New Culture—New People

Another thing that I often tell people, especially students, when it comes to studying abroad is that it is an excellent choice for getting familiar with a new culture and people. Do not look at your chance of studying abroad as something you are doing for education. Think of it as a holiday, and you will realize how quickly the experience changes.

You will get to immerse yourself in an entirely new culture and be with people from all parts of the world. For anyone who wants to understand the world around them and its inhabitants better, studying abroad is definitely something that one needs to look into.

Career Opportunities

Aside from getting access to a great education, another great thing about studying abroad is that you get access to many career opportunities. Most of us tend to pursue a better education to enter into better careers, which is exactly what studying abroad will provide us with.

No matter the field you are pursuing, a shot at a good career is always something that comes with being in institutes that are recognized the world over.

Personal Growth

For many of us, personal growth is essential. Without it, we struggle to process experiences and understand life as it should be. Living in a new country among strangers teaches invaluable lessons in independence and resilience.

Studying abroad is an excellent opportunity for those seeking personal development and a chance to grow into stronger, more self-sufficient individuals. While the transition may be challenging at first, the most rewarding experiences often come from overcoming difficulties.

Despite its many benefits, convincing students to step out of their comfort zones and leave home isn't easy without strong reasoning.

When considering studying abroad, there are three key stages at which you can pursue it: during school, during undergraduate studies, or after graduation.

This is another area that confuses many students, but we're here to simplify it by outlining the advantages of studying abroad at both the undergraduate and graduate levels.

Our goal is to provide you with a clear understanding so you don't feel lost while deciding your path as an aspiring international student.

Benefits of Studying Abroad for School Students

Perhaps the greatest exposure a person can gain comes from studying abroad as a school student. However, this decision is not entirely autonomous, as convincing your parents plays a significant role in the process.

That said, studying abroad at a young age offers numerous benefits. Here are some key advantages to consider:

New Perspective

Studying abroad is an excellent opportunity for school students, as it provides access to new perspectives and ways of thinking.

At this stage, students are still shaping their thoughts and worldviews. Exposure to an international education system and diverse cultures can significantly broaden their horizons, fostering personal growth and a more global mindset.

Finding Your Calling

Another significant benefit of studying abroad as a school student is the opportunity to discover your true calling.

If you've been searching for your identity, strengths, or passions, studying in a new environment can provide the clarity you need. Many students find their path in arts, sports, or other fields because their international school encourages and nurtures their talents, helping them grow in ways they may not have experienced otherwise.

Building New Relations

Another great advantage of studying abroad as a school student is the opportunity to build lasting relationships. The friends and connections you make during this time can become some of your closest allies for all the right reasons.

At a young age, many students studying away from home experience vulnerability and face the world in entirely new ways. The challenges can feel overwhelming, but this shared experience often brings people closer together. As a result, the bonds formed during these years tend to be strong and long-lasting.

Becoming Better Humans

Another key advantage of international education is that it helps shape individuals into better human beings overall.

Studying abroad exposes you to diverse knowledge, perspectives, and ways of thinking. The more you engage with different cultures, the more you learn to adapt, embrace new ideas, and even make necessary compromises.

Ultimately, international education at the school level fosters personal growth in ways that many people struggle to achieve even after years of traditional schooling.

Benefits of Studying Abroad for Undergraduate Students

The life of an undergraduate student can be summed up in one word—**adventurous**. For many, this stage marks a transition into a completely different lifestyle, one that can shape their future in profound ways. It is a time of growth, challenges, and self-discovery.

If you choose to pursue your undergraduate studies abroad, the good news is that you will gain invaluable experiences that not only enrich your personal and academic journey but also open doors to greater opportunities in the future.

It Teaches You a Lot

Going abroad for a diploma or bachelor's degree is not an easy decision for everyone. It means leaving the comfort of home for two, three, or even four years—stepping out of a familiar environment and into uncharted territory.

As a young person, you will learn to manage tasks that once seemed simple, such as opening a bank account, handling finances, buying groceries, and paying utility bills. These everyday responsibilities will foster independence and resilience.

If you are new to the country and unfamiliar with its native language, the experience will be even more challenging. However, despite the difficulties, this journey will ultimately shape you into a stronger, more capable version of yourself.

A Great Way to Learn New Skills

The main advantage of studying abroad is the opportunity to develop valuable skills that you might have missed out on if you had chosen a different path. Being in an unfamiliar country requires you to adapt—embracing different cultures, building friendships with people from diverse backgrounds, and navigating new social dynamics.

At first, these cross-cultural communication skills may seem like just a necessity, but in the long run, they will prove invaluable—especially if you aspire to work in the international job market.

There is a lot to Learn.

Studying abroad exposes you to an entirely new educational system, giving you the opportunity to explore and refine the craft you are most passionate about. Undergraduate degrees serve as the foundation for future success, and having a diverse range of academic choices allows you to discover your true calling.

Additionally, the grading system and academic expectations may differ from what you are used to, presenting new challenges that push you to grow. Embracing these challenges will not only enhance your skills but also help you become a more adaptable and well-rounded student.

A Great Way of Expanding the Network

Another significant benefit of studying internationally as an undergraduate student is the opportunity to expand your network. You will meet people from diverse backgrounds and build meaningful relationships that can stand the test of time.

This expanded network is invaluable—not only for personal growth but also for future opportunities. Whether you pursue a career or further studies, the connections you make during your undergraduate years can open doors and provide support in the global job market.

Traveling, Cultures, Traditions, and Languages

As an undergraduate student studying abroad, you become more curious and open to learning about things you might not have paid much attention to otherwise.

Traveling becomes a significant part of the experience, as you may explore different cities or regions to gain a deeper understanding of their history and culture. Likewise, you'll be exposed to new traditions and ways of life. While adapting may seem challenging at first, the more time you spend immersing yourself, the more natural it becomes. Keeping an open mind will help you avoid isolation and make the most of your journey.

Lastly, learning new languages and recognizing their importance as an undergraduate student is an incredibly rewarding experience. While it takes time and effort, the personal and professional benefits make it all worthwhile.

How Graduate-Level Students Can Benefit from Studying Abroad

Life often leads us to pursue local education for our undergraduate studies, but that doesn't mean the opportunity to study abroad is lost. Many students assume that if they miss their chance as undergraduates, they cannot study internationally at the graduate level—but that is far from the truth.

Numerous universities offer graduate-level programs for international students, providing another opportunity to gain global exposure and advanced education. If studying abroad is your goal, I highly encourage you to read on and explore the possibilities available to you.

1. You Get to Experience New Teaching Styles

Experiencing different teaching styles is an invaluable part of studying abroad, whether at the undergraduate or graduate level. Each educational system has its own approach, allowing students to adapt and grow in new ways.

The key takeaway is that studying abroad exposes you to diverse learning methods. If you want to enhance your ability to learn through various approaches, this experience will refine your skills and help you develop a more adaptable and well-rounded academic mindset.

2. Shot at a Great Career

Another significant benefit of studying abroad as a graduate student is the opportunity to build a strong career. You gain access to new job markets and workplaces where you can showcase your adaptability and ability to thrive in diverse environments—qualities that impress employers.

Many companies actively seek graduates with international exposure, as they bring valuable transferable skills such as cultural awareness, problem-solving, and independence. Even at the graduate level, studying abroad provides excellent career prospects as long as you are focused and determined to make the most of your opportunities.

3. Confidence Development and Personal Growth

Confidence development and personal growth are lifelong processes. Even if you missed the opportunity to study abroad as an undergraduate, you can still focus on building these qualities at the graduate level.

Studying abroad helps you develop essential skills in areas such as leadership, communication, and cross-cultural awareness. These experiences not only contribute to personal growth but also enhance your confidence, preparing you to navigate diverse professional and social environments with ease.

4. Meeting New People and Learning New Things

You are never too old to meet new people and learn new things. Even as a graduate student studying abroad, you have the opportunity to form meaningful connections and gain valuable experiences that enhance your communication, understanding, and ability to relate to others.

Stepping into unfamiliar territory broadens your horizons, allowing you to explore new perspectives and opportunities.

When applying to international universities, you will likely need to take specific tests as part of the admission requirements. Many students see these exams as obstacles, fearing they might hinder their plans. However, these tests often seem more daunting by name than in reality—they are structured assessments designed to evaluate fundamental skills.

Below, you'll find a list of tests that may be required based on your area of study and chosen university. Keep in mind that not all tests apply to every program, so you won't need to take all of them.

- **IELTS**: IELTS, or the **International English Language Testing System**, is an international standardized English language proficiency test for non-native English speakers. The British Council, IELTS Australia, and Cambridge Assessment English manage IELTS. There are two IELTS tests available – IELTS Academic, which measures the level of English proficiency suitable for an academic environment, and IELTS General Training, which measures English proficiency in everyday context. The test assesses an individual's listening, reading, writing, and speaking skills.

- **TOEFL**: TOEFL, or **Test of English as a Foreign Language**, is a standardized test used to measure the English language ability of non-native speakers looking forward to enrolling in English-speaking institutes. The test is valid for over 11,000 universities spread across 190 countries. Like IELTS, TOEFL is also used to assess an individual's reading, writing, listening, and speaking ability.

- **PTE**: PTE or **Pearson Test of English** is a computer-based academic English test for non-native speakers looking to study abroad.

- **CAE**: CAE or **Certificate in Advanced English** is a test that often serves as an alternative to IELTS. It is managed by Cambridge ESOL and is accepted in nearly every university and college in the UK. It is also accepted in institutions in Australia and other countries. Like all the tests previously mentioned, this one also involves reading, writing, listening, and speaking.

In addition to the tests, there are some entrance tests that one might have to take depending on the program they choose.

- **SAT**: SAT is a standardized test widely used for college admissions in the United States. It is a multiple-choice test created and administered by the College Board. The test mainly looks at mathematical skills and evidence-based reading and writing, lasting 3 hours. The highest SAT score is 1,600, with 1,060 being the average.

- **ACT**: Similar to SAT, ACT is also a standardized test that is used for college admissions in the United States. The test covers four academic skills: English, mathematics, reading, and scientific reasoning. It also has writing as an optional section that some colleges require.

- **GRE**: GRE, or the Graduate Record Examinations, is another form of standardized test that is an admission requirement for several graduate schools in the United States, Canada, and a few other countries. The test is essential for master's or doctoral degree programs, with the test being valid in over 160 countries worldwide. The test is 3 hours and 45 minutes long, with a 1-minute break after completing each section and a 10-minute break after the third section.

- **GMAT**: GMAT or Graduate Management Admission Test is a computer adaptive test that assesses analytical, writing, quantitative, verbal, and reading skills in written English, and it is a prerequisite for graduate management programs such as MBA. The test is mainly there to assess an individual's critical thinking skills. Knowing how to reason through the provided information and analyze it allows for a great GMAT score.

Chapter 2

How To Choose the Right Program

Preparing for major exams like engineering, CAT, GRE, MBA, GMAT, TOEFL, and civil service requires a significant investment of both time and money. These life-changing tests often demand years of preparation. For example, securing a top degree from institutions like IIT/IIM in India typically involves two to three years of rigorous classes and practice, with an initial investment of approximately two to three million rupees.

Similarly, in the United States, pursuing an MBA from a renowned university can cost up to $150,000. Despite the high costs, students make these investments because they believe quality education is the key to a brighter future. Given the stakes, making the right decision about your chosen program is crucial.

If you are considering studying in Australia, it is important to stay informed about recent developments. The Department of Home Affairs has released a report on the country's visa programs, which provides valuable insights. Between 2021 and 2022, approximately 230,000 student visas were granted. However, less than 40 percent of these were issued to students from leading countries returning to Australia between November 2021 and May 2022.

Below is a breakdown of student visa statistics for various countries.

India	34,035
China	25,689
Nepal	18,889
Vietnam	7,172

Lodgments for student visas in Australia peaked at 473,415 in 2018–2019 before dropping to 262,633 in 2020–2021 due to the

COVID-19 pandemic. However, by May 2022, applications had surged again, reaching 314,388.

If you are applying for a student visa, it is essential to keep key dates in mind. Australia's fiscal year ends on June 30, but the country reopened its borders to international students on December 15, 2021, after an extended closure due to the pandemic. These changes affected student mobility between December 2021 and May 2022.

A similar trend is seen in China's student visa applications. Between 2018 and 2019, 91,296 applications were lodged, but this number fell to 52,041 in 2020–2021 before recovering slightly to 55,601 by May 2022—only 60 percent of pre-pandemic levels.

Indian applicants also saw a decline, with visa applications dropping from 89,868 in 2018–2019 to 57,635 in 2021–2022, returning to 64 percent of pre-pandemic volumes. Meanwhile, Nepalese students reached 90 percent of pre-pandemic levels, with applications falling from 43,190 in 2018–2019 to 39,066 in 2021–2022.

Additionally, the Australian government has released details regarding international students' study and work rights upon arrival.

In the United States, Indian applications for master's programs increased by 36 percent in 2021 compared to 2019, with first-time enrollments for Indian students surging by an astounding 430 percent.

Under New Zealand's revised laws, degree-level students remain eligible for study work rights. However, non-degree students can only work after their studies if their qualifications align with an occupation listed on the Green List, which identifies areas experiencing labor shortages. These students can only pursue careers supported by the Green List.

New Zealand's Green List currently includes 85 occupations, providing a streamlined pathway to residency for skilled professionals, including healthcare providers, engineers, tech experts, and trade workers. Additionally, graduate students are eligible for three years of post-graduate employment in the country.

However, international students will not be permitted to apply for a second work permit. This policy aims to reduce the time a person can work in New Zealand without applying for an Accredited Employer Work Visa, which requires employers to first check for available New Zealand citizens to fill a position.

Financial Requirements for Studying in New Zealand

Moving to New Zealand for studies requires extensive financial resources. Beyond the 5,000 students under the "cohort 4" designation, all international students must provide proof of additional funds to cover accommodation and living costs.

- Higher education and English-speaking students must show ownership of assets worth NZD 20,000 per year.

- Primary and secondary students must prove assets worth NZD 17,000 per year.

- Previously, the financial requirement for all levels of study was NZD 15,000 annually.

Additionally, international students must pay their full tuition fees for the first year upfront. If enrolling in a short-term program, students must pay for the entire program upfront.

Students seeking to transfer into a work permit must also provide proof of funds worth NZD 5,000.

A recent survey showed that approximately three-quarters of agents reported an increase in student interest in New Zealand over the past two months compared to other countries.

More than half of the agents strongly agreed that student interest in New Zealand had increased, marking a significant shift from October 2021, when only 28 percent of surveyed agents believed Australia had a competitive edge in attracting international students.

According to Navitas, Australia has significantly closed the gap between the UK and Canada in terms of international student enrollment. Students from South and Southeast Asia have shown the most interest, with nearly 90 percent of agents in those regions reporting a surge in student interest in studying in Australia over the past two months.

Why Australia is Attracting More International Students

Neil Fitzroy, General Manager for Global Recruitment UPA Navitas, highlighted key reasons for Australia's growing appeal:

- A substantial rise in international student travel for Australia's mid-year intake

- Increased energy and engagement on campuses across the country, fueling future admissions

- A shift in sentiment among international students, driven by confidence in Australia's handling of COVID-19

- A fully vaccinated adult population exceeding 95 percent, with safety measures still in place

As a result, Australia's global market share in education is expected to expand, particularly in categories targeting international students.

Canada's Expansion of International Student Opportunities

Canada is also increasing its intake of international students, particularly through higher caps in the "Federal High Skilled" category for international graduates from Canadian institutions. The number of slots in this category will increase from 55,900 to 111,500 by 2024. Immigration programs supporting this expansion include:

- Federal Skilled Worker Program (FSWP)

- Federal Skilled Trades Program (FSTP)

- Canadian Experience Class (CEC)

Canada's New Immigration Priorities

Canada's new immigration targets focus on two key priorities:

1. Attracting top-tier students and workers to strengthen the Canadian labor market

2. Assisting refugees, particularly from Afghanistan, in building a safer life in Canada

Canada's Immigration Minister, Marc Miller, explained to CIC News that these revised policies balance the country's economic needs with its international responsibilities. The changes aim to address labor shortages, reunite families, and support vulnerable populations through refugee programs.

Canada remains committed to supporting its economic development by increasing the retention of newcomers in regions facing economic, labor, and demographic challenges. The country takes pride in its immigration achievements and continues to welcome international students, aiming to become a top destination for higher education.

Immigration as a Key Driver of Canada's Economy

Canada's immigration policies are designed to promote maximum workforce participation, recognizing immigration as a critical factor in sustaining economic growth. According to the Canadian government, immigration accounts for nearly 100% of labor force growth. With five million Canadians expected to retire by the end of the decade, the worker-to-retiree ratio is projected to drop to 3:1, highlighting the urgent need for increased immigration.

In response, Canada introduced a new immigration stream targeting international workers and students specializing in sectors with significant labor shortages.

Temporary to Permanent Residence Stream (TR2PR)

The TR2PR policy, introduced by Minister of Immigration, Refugees, and Citizenship Marco Mendicino, aims to address labor gaps and recognize the critical contributions of new arrivals during the pandemic.

This policy benefits individuals with temporary resident status, allowing them to build a long-term future in Canada while playing an essential role in the country's economic recovery and development. Canada values international students not just for their temporary presence but for their lasting impact on the economy and workforce.

Pathways to Permanent Residency for International Students

International students make up more than half of Canada's new permanent residents. To accommodate foreign students, Canadian immigration authorities have reduced spaces in the Express Entry stream to prioritize international students under the TR2PR stream.

This is a progressive step toward welcoming more students who are deciding when and what to study in Canada. However, the TR2PR stream specifically targets certain sectors and occupations, allowing international students to align their studies with in-demand fields, enhancing their chances of securing permanent residency and employment in Canada.

Additionally, the Provincial Nominee Program, a key pathway for international students to migrate to Canada, will expand its capacity from 83,500 in 2022 to 93,000 in 2024. Despite favorable policies, the Canadian immigration process remains slow and frustrating. Delays and unpredictability have caused significant concern among visa applicants seeking permanent residency, an issue that has persisted for some time.

A similar trend is evident in the number of visas issued to international students. In 2018 and 2019, visa approvals were at a peak of 405,742 but dropped significantly to 232,750 in 2020 and 2021. By 2021 and 2022, approvals had recovered to 56% of pre-pandemic levels, with 228,150 visas granted. As of June 2022, there were 469,306 Canadian student visa holders globally, with approximately three-quarters (354,475 students) residing in Canada, while the remaining 114,831 were based outside the country. Students outside Canada are eligible to travel if they are fully vaccinated.

Australian state governments, a coalition of eight research universities, and universities across the country sought to strengthen ties with India—the second-largest source of international students in 2022—ahead of the upcoming February intake.

Between January and July 2023, the number of international students enrolled in Australian courses reached 710,893, reflecting a 34% increase compared to the same period the previous year. It is important to note that this figure represents a headcount, including all students holding a student visa during the reference period. A student may be counted across multiple years if their course extends beyond a single year.

In addition to the headcount, international student enrolments and commencements track the actual educational activities undertaken by students on student visas. Since students may enroll in multiple courses across different sectors during the reference period, the enrolment and commencement figures will always exceed the student headcount.

Furthermore, it is important to acknowledge the transition from a state-based registration system for education providers to a nationally recognized system. During this period, there were instances where the study location of certain students could not be determined, and in such cases, a "Multi-State" designation was assigned.

New Zealand's immigration reforms reflect the government's commitment to aligning immigration policies with economic priorities, particularly by streamlining the flow of low-skilled labor out of the country.

International students wishing to study in the UK must obtain a Tier 4 student visa, which is available for full-time university students pursuing a degree. This visa does not permit students enrolled in short-term or language courses to reside in the UK. Applicants must be at least 16 years old and have an offer from a licensed student sponsor. Additionally, they must demonstrate sufficient financial resources to support themselves and cover tuition fees, with the required amount varying based on individual circumstances. International students must also meet English language proficiency requirements in speaking, reading, writing, and comprehension.

When considering studying abroad, prospective students should evaluate a country's educational programs, financial requirements, visa processes, and overall stance on immigration. It is advisable to choose a destination that offers a pathway to permanent residency upon completing one's studies.

According to the ICEF Survey, the cost of living is the most significant factor influencing international students' choice of study destination.

Chapter 3

Finding the Right Funding Sources

Going abroad to study is an exceptional idea, but you might hesitate due to a big glaring issue: funding.

You might wonder why securing sufficient funding for a high-quality education is so challenging. For most students, studying in one of the world's leading countries is an opportunity that is hard to pass up. However, skyrocketing tuition fees, travel expenses, and lodging costs often prevent them from pursuing this dream. Fortunately, all is not lost—various scholarship programs can help meet funding requirements and reduce reliance on student loans.

To select the most suitable scholarship program, it is essential to understand why students face financial barriers when applying to study abroad. The most significant expense is often tuition fees at prestigious universities. High-quality education comes at a substantial cost, and international students typically pay higher tuition fees than domestic students. In the United States, undergraduate tuition averages between $26,000 and $35,000 per year, while postgraduate studies range from $40,000 to $50,000 annually.

To determine eligibility for scholarships, you can complete an eligibility questionnaire, which assesses whether you meet the necessary criteria. This questionnaire evaluates:

- Your country of citizenship

- The duration of your residency in your home country

- Your work experience

- Whether scholarships are available for students from your country

Completing the eligibility questionnaire is a prerequisite for applying for a scholarship.

Beyond tuition, the next major challenge for international students is the high cost of living. In many developed countries, living expenses far exceed an international student's typical budget. These costs include food, accommodation, transportation, and other daily necessities, which fluctuate monthly and can add up quickly. In Europe, the average monthly cost of living ranges from €700 to €1,000, while in the U.S., expenses rise even higher, averaging between $1,200 and $1,500 per month. These costs can be significantly higher in major metropolitan areas or business hubs like New York and Los Angeles.

In addition to living expenses, flights, and visa applications can strain an international student's finances even before they arrive in a new country. These costs largely depend on the destination, as airfare can be particularly expensive for some locations. If you plan to study in a developed country like the United States, you must also factor in the cost of a student visa, which averages around $160.

Once you reach your destination with hopes for a brighter future, additional academic expenses, such as textbooks and study materials, can further impact your budget. You might not expect it, but textbooks can be a significant expense. Costs vary by course, and some programs require students to purchase specific books, which may not always be affordable. Another important consideration is the rise of e-learning and digital education. Not all students have the financial means to purchase laptops or access printers for assignments.

After identifying these financial challenges, you can explore funding options that best suit your situation. Many study-abroad programs provide financial support tailored to students from specific countries. The key to selecting the right program is understanding the scholarship policies of your chosen study destination.

One of the primary funding options is applying for financial aid. If you are a U.S. citizen, you may qualify for federal financial aid, which includes grants, loans, and work-study programs. If you prefer not to pursue public funding, you can explore scholarships and grants offered by private organizations, foundations, or financial aid offices. International students can also apply for global financial aid programs, though eligibility requirements may be restrictive.

Beyond financial aid, scholarships and international educational grants are excellent funding alternatives. Numerous institutions and organizations offer scholarship programs specifically designed for international students. The best way to find these opportunities is through online research or by consulting your school's academic counselors. However, the most effective approach is reaching out to study-abroad offices, which can provide a comprehensive list of available scholarships and grants. Countries such as the United States, Australia, and the United Kingdom offer some of the best scholarship programs for international students.

Another effective option for securing additional funding is taking out student loans. Student loans are considered one of the most viable financial tools for covering international education costs and related expenses. They offer several advantages, including low and affordable interest rates, extended repayment periods, and deferred payment options. Students can apply for loans through government-funded institutions or private organizations. However, student loan debt can become a significant burden after graduation, with many borrowers struggling to repay their loans in full over their lifetime.

The top scholarship programs that offer the most generous funding for international students include:

1. Fulbright Scholarships (USA)

The Fulbright Scholarship is a prestigious program funded by the U.S. government. It is awarded to non-U.S. students worldwide who wish to pursue a master's degree or Ph.D. in the United States.

2. Chevening Scholarships (UK)

The Chevening Scholarship is a fully funded scholarship program offered to international students from over 160 countries who want to earn a master's degree in the United Kingdom. It is one of the world's most renowned and cut-throat scholarship programs.

3. Eiffel Excellence Scholarship Program (France)

If you plan to study in France, you may be eligible for the Eiffel Excellence Scholarship Program (EESP). Designed for international students pursuing a master's degree or Ph.D. in France, this scholarship prioritizes academic excellence and cultural diversity.

4. DAAD Scholarships (Germany):

The DAAD scholarship is a government-funded scholarship program offered by Germany, and it is awarded to international students from all over the world who want to pursue an academic degree in Germany. It is one of the most popular and attainable scholarships for international students.

5. Emerging Leaders in the Americas Program

The Emerging Leaders in the Americas Program provides students from Latin America and the Caribbean with short-term exchange opportunities for study or research at Canadian post-secondary institutions.

6. Canada-CARICOM Skills Training for the Green Economy Scholarships

The Canada-CARICOM Skills Training for the Green Economy Scholarships provide students from the Caribbean Community (CARICOM) member states with short-term exchange opportunities at publicly funded Canadian colleges and institutes.

Beyond these programs, scholarship opportunities vary by country. Canada is recognized as a global leader in education and scholarships, offering numerous programs to help international students secure suitable grants and financial aid. The Canadian government actively participates in international scholarship initiatives through Global Affairs Canada. These include scholarships provided by the Canadian government, foreign governments, non-governmental organizations, and international institutions.

The Study in Canada Scholarships program offers short-term exchange opportunities for international students from newly eligible countries and territories. These scholarships support students at Canadian post-secondary institutions, including colleges, undergraduate, and graduate programs, for study and research.

The Government of Ontario, in partnership with WeRPN, has established the BEGIN program, which serves as a bridge for Personal Support Workers (PSWs) and Registered Practical Nurses (RPNs) to explore various career pathways in Long-Term Care (LTC) and Home and Community Care (HCC). Students enrolled in accredited PSW-to-RPN or RPN-to-RN programs may qualify for tuition grants through this initiative. The program also connects graduates with significant employment opportunities in Ontario's LTC and HCC sectors. Eligible PSWs can receive tuition reimbursements of up to $6,000 per year (with a maximum of $15,000), while eligible RPNs can receive up to $10,000 per year (with a maximum of $30,000).

Additionally, the Canada-CARICOM Skills Training for the Green Economy Scholarships provides short-term exchange opportunities at publicly funded Canadian colleges and institutes for students from Caribbean Community (CARICOM) member states. The Emerging Leaders in the Americas Program offers similar short-term exchange opportunities for students from Latin America and the Caribbean to study or conduct research at Canadian post-secondary institutions.

If you are considering Australia for higher education, the Australia Awards is one of the most prestigious scholarship programs. This initiative promotes knowledge-sharing, educational networks, and long-term connections between Australia and its neighboring countries through extensive scholarship opportunities.

In 2022, the Department of Foreign Affairs and Trade (DFAT) awarded 2,075 Australia Awards scholarships and short courses to individuals from 27 developing countries, with an estimated investment of $200 million. The Australian government's development policy—Australian Aid: Promoting Prosperity, Reducing Poverty, and Enhancing Stability—recognizes tertiary education as a critical component of sustainable development.

Australia Awards Short Courses are intensive training programs designed to address specific technical or soft skills gaps. These short courses, typically lasting less than three months, are delivered by approved Australian higher education providers or Australian Registered Training Organizations (RTOs) in Australia or partner countries. DFAT's overseas posts manage and administer these programs.

The Australia Awards program integrates scholarships funded by DFAT, the Department of Education, and the Australian Centre for International Agricultural Research (ACIAR).

Another excellent scholarship option for studying in Australia is the Destination Australia Program (DAP). This initiative, funded by the Australian government, provides scholarships through qualified tertiary education institutions for both domestic and international students to study in regional Australia. Destination Australia scholarships offer up to $15,000 per student per year for a wide range of degrees, from Certificate IV programs to Ph.D. studies. This funding is available for up to four years at regional campuses across Australia.

Additionally, many Provider Scholarships are available through Australian universities and institutions based on academic merit. Prospective students should consult the admissions department or international office at their chosen institution for specific details and eligibility requirements.

Scholarship Opportunities in New Zealand

For those not considering Australia, New Zealand also offers excellent scholarship programs and grants for international students. The New Zealand Scholarships for the 2023–2024 academic term are currently open, with approximately 5,000 fully funded scholarships available. These scholarships support international students pursuing Bachelor's, Master's, Ph.D., and Postdoctoral degree programs. Most of these scholarships are funded by the Government of New Zealand.

New Zealand boasts an outstanding education system with internationally recognized qualifications. One of the key advantages of studying in New Zealand is that students are not required to remain or return to the country for work after completing their degrees. Applications for Fully Funded Scholarships in New Zealand must be submitted online.

International students can apply for New Zealand Government Visa Sponsorship Jobs, providing opportunities to work while studying. The New Zealand Scholarship has a duration of four years for undergraduate programs, while master's students receive funding for up to two years. All programs under this scholarship are taught in English, making New Zealand an attractive destination for international students.

With only eight universities in New Zealand, the number of applicants remains relatively low, increasing the chances of acceptance and securing grants. One notable program is the University of Auckland International Student Excellence Scholarship, designed for international undergraduate and graduate students. This scholarship offers up to $10,000 toward compulsory tuition fees and is awarded for a duration of two years, with up to 50 scholarships granted annually.

The New Zealand Government Scholarships support undergraduate, master's, and doctoral degree programs. These scholarships are available to eligible citizens from developing countries, allowing them to study at a New Zealand university or a Pacific university.

Additional Scholarship Programs in New Zealand

Short-Term Training Scholarships for Pacific and Timor-Leste Citizens – Provides short-term grants for skills training and on-the-job work experience for workers from eligible Pacific countries and Timor-Leste.

Short-Term Training Scholarships for Southeast Asia and Timor-Leste Citizens – Offers short-term scholarships for workers from eligible Southeast Asian countries and Timor-Leste to gain specialized skills training.

English Language Training for Officials Scholarships (NZELTO) – A short-term scholarship for government officials from eligible African and Asian countries to travel to New Zealand for English language training.

University-Specific Scholarships

- University of Otago Scholarships – Open for international applicants at any time, with no specific deadline. Otago University offers 200 doctoral scholarships for both domestic and international students. Those pursuing professional doctorates or Ph.D. programs are eligible to apply.

- Wellington Scholarships – Available for any program at the university, including doctoral programs, these scholarships provide substantial financial support for academic advancement.

Chapter 4

Studying in the USA

The decision to pursue a degree in the United States is a defining moment in your personal, academic, and career goals.

The Institute of International Education (IIE) states that more than 1.1 million students are inclined toward earning an advanced degree in the United States. There are various reasons, including a spectrum of opportunities. However, weighing the pros and cons of moving to a new country can be intimidating.

Before deciding to study at a college or university in the USA, carefully consider the advantages, challenges, and opportunities to make an informed decision for your future.

Studying in the U.S. provides access to advanced language skills and valuable intercultural experiences within a leading global higher education system featuring cutting-edge technology and research. This will enhance your comprehension, problem-solving abilities, and understanding of modern practices in your field.

U.S. higher education is known for its diverse degree options, allowing students to select programs aligned with their interests and career goals, which may not be available elsewhere.

For students from developing nations with limited resources, studying in the U.S. offers access to extensive academic and professional resources that foster learning, growth, and skill development, improving their standing in the global job market.

Many U.S. universities offer a wide array of elective and complementary courses, often in collaboration with other regional institutions or consortia, enabling students to explore subjects beyond their major and enrich their academic experience.

Even if you don't plan to immigrate, studying and working in the U.S. can boost your employability in your home country, particularly with multinational companies. International students can gain real-world experience through experiential learning, co-op programs, and internships, building connections with potential employers who might later sponsor work visas.

For STEM degree students, the U.S. offers further benefits. They can extend their stay for an additional two years beyond the standard one-year post-graduation period if employed by a U.S. company. F-1 students with STEM degrees from SEVP-certified universities can apply for Optional Practical Training (OPT), allowing them to work in the U.S. for a total of 36 months to gain practical, paid experience in their field.

For non-native English speakers, studying in the U.S. provides full language immersion, refining their skills and offering a competitive edge in the job market. Multilingualism is a valuable asset, demonstrating strong cross-cultural communication skills sought by employers.

Attending an American university also allows students to expand their global network, experience new cultures, and develop a broader international perspective.

The United States is a diverse environment with various cultures, races, and ethnicities, fostering acceptance across communities. As a large country with diverse landscapes, cultures, and experiences, studying in the U.S. offers numerous opportunities for travel and exploration.

Now, let's explore the top universities in the United States.

Massachusetts Institute of Technology (MIT)

The Massachusetts Institute of Technology (MIT) is a world-renowned university dedicated to advancing education in science, technology, and related fields that shape the modern world. It has produced some of the brightest minds, including Nobel Prize-winning physicist Richard Feynman, former Italian Prime Minister Mario Draghi, and acclaimed architect I. M. Pei.

Harvard University

Harvard University is a private Ivy League research university in Cambridge, Massachusetts. It is the oldest institution of higher learning in the United States and one of the world's most prestigious and highly-ranked universities.

Stanford University

Located near Palo Alto, California, Stanford University is a world-class institution renowned for its excellence in STEM programs. It has produced numerous Nobel Prize winners, Turing Award recipients, and Fields Medalists. Notable Stanford alumni include billionaire venture capitalist Peter Thiel, Instagram cofounder Kevin Systrom, U.S. Senator Cory Booker, and the first female U.S. Supreme Court Justice, Sandra Day O'Connor.

University of California, Berkeley

The University of California, Berkeley, is renowned for driving technological and social change. Its faculty has contributed to groundbreaking discoveries, including the identification of Vitamins E and K, the development of the atomic bomb, and the creation of the flu vaccine. UC Berkeley houses over 150 departments and eight interdisciplinary research facilities across five colleges. Additionally, its esteemed faculty includes four Pulitzer Prize winners.

Princeton University

The fourth oldest college is a leading private research university. Princeton shows commitment to service through learning and professional and community connections. Princeton has produced 21 Rhodes scholars over the last ten years and has produced 18 total alumni Nobel Prize winners.

Columbia University

Upper Manhattan, Columbia's crown jewel, is an Ivy League University. This school's location helps provide students with a wealth of resources and learning opportunities. Columbia has produced more Nobel Laureates than any other university in the Ivy League. Columbia alums include five founding fathers, 34 presidents, prime ministers, and nine Supreme Court justices.

Let's go over the school entry requirements for U.S. universities.

Academic Qualifications

You need to have good grades in your previous academic record, equivalent to the minimum Grade Point Average (GPA) for entry to your program of choice.

English Language Requirements

With advanced English language proficiency, you will have the necessary background to start a bachelor's or master's degree immediately. Generally, scores from any of the following English language exams are accepted:

1. TOEFL (Test of English as a Foreign Language)

2. Kaplan iBT

3. IELTS (International English Language Testing System)

4. IELTS Indicator

5. Pearson Test of English (PTE)

6. Duolingo English Test (DET)

A college major is a specific subject area that students specialize in. Typically, between one-third and one-half of the courses you'll take in college will be in your major related to it. You can choose one of the following majors:

Arts and Humanities

Programs in art and humanities take a multidisciplinary approach to education. They combine the study of languages, literature, art, music, philosophy, and religion.

Business

Business programs involve teaching students the skills and operations of the business industry. They include studies in various areas, including accountancy, finance, marketing, human resources, economics, etc.

Health and Medicine

Programs in health and medicine focus on the study, research, and knowledge of health principles and the application of corresponding expertise to prevent, diagnose, and care for humans and animals.

Public and Social Services

Students learn to analyze, manage, and provide public programs and services in this study area. Areas of focus include law and legal studies, public administration, social services, protective services, and more.

Science, Technology, Engineering, and Math

Programs in STEM include majors in four disciplines: Science, technology, engineering, and math. The skills needed for each domain overlap, and studies in these fields provide students with a multidisciplinary skill set.

Social Sciences

This field of study is where students learn how to focus on how individuals behave within society, how society works, and the relationship between the two.

U.S Scholarships for International Students

Scholarships or funding opportunities can be invaluable for students aspiring to study in the United States.

The first step towards availing a funding opportunity is to contact your school's financial aid office. Various colleges offer scholarship programs specifically for international students attending their institutions.

Most scholarship programs require you to complete an application form, others require a specific written piece of work, while some require you to pursue studies in a particular field.

Once you have secured admission to your university of choice, you will need to get all your documents in order.

These include:

- Passport

- Curriculum Vitae/résumé

- Certificates of graduation

- Letters of recommendation

- Transcripts

- Scorecards for entrance exams

- Scores on your English Proficiency Test

- Work experience letters

- Statement of Purpose (SOP)

- Essays

- Evidence of funds

- Proposal for Research

- Certificates for extracurricular activities

- Copy of the application of confirmation

Post-Graduate Visa Options for International Students

If you decide to stay and work in the United States after completing your degree. There are a few visa options available to you. Some of them are discussed below:

Practical Training on an F1 Visa

An F1 student is generally entitled to a year of post-graduation practical training. Authorization for this type of training may be granted for 12 months. The department that deals with international students at your university will inform you of all the different training options available. You can also apply for an extension if you are in a STEM field.

Non-Immigrant H-3 Visa

An H-3 visa is tailored for those individuals who do not have the relevant education or work experience. It is for students interested in coming to the U.S. to train in a particular field with the intention of transporting that knowledge back to their home country upon completing their visa.

Non-Immigrant H-1B Visa (Specialty Occupation)

To obtain this type of visa, you need to be:

A U.S employer to sponsor the applicant

A U.S bachelor's degree holder or an equivalent

A correlation between the job duties and the applicant's education and work experience

The H-1B visa is granted for an initial period of 3 years and can be given an extension for another three years, but it cannot be extended for more than six years.

Employment-Based Immigration

To obtain an employment-based immigration visa, an applicant must apply for a specific labor certification. This is often a strenuous process and may take years, based on jurisdiction.

Advanced Degree Professions

Applicants with advanced degrees (Master's or Bachelor's, plus five years of work experience) can apply for this category.

An F1 visa holder can secure a PR/citizenship if they receive an employer sponsorship, marry a US citizen, seek asylum, win the green card lottery, receive sponsorship from a relative who owns a business, participate in military service, or receive a parent or child sponsorship.

Job Opportunities for Students in the United States

Many part-time jobs are available for students who want to work while studying. The highest-paying roles often include campus ambassador, barista, teaching assistant, library assistant, receptionist, research or study assistant, department assistant, catering assistant, sales assistant, or tutor/peer mentor.

The federal minimum wage is $7.25 per hour, but state laws vary, so your study location will significantly affect your potential income.

International students with F-1 visas typically can work on campus at their university for a maximum of 20 hours per week during academic terms. This can increase to 40 hours per week during holidays.

So, prepare to begin your journey, apply to your chosen university, and get ready for a potentially life-changing opportunity!

Tuition Fee

Tuition fees will likely be a student's primary and largest expense. However, the exact amount varies significantly based on the course, university type (public or private), and any scholarships awarded. Public universities are generally less expensive but more competitive to enter than private institutions. Prospective students should research the tuition fees of their intended programs. Estimated annual costs range from USD 8,000 to USD 55,000, with undergraduate programs costing approximately $20,000 to $40,000, graduate programs $20,000 to $45,000, and doctoral programs $28,000 to $55,000. Community colleges typically cost between $6,000 and $20,000 per year, while English language courses can range from $700 to $2,000 monthly.

Generally, humanities and education courses are less expensive, while specialized fields like engineering and medicine, including MBA programs, tend to be more costly. Postgraduate studies are typically more expensive per year than undergraduate programs but are shorter in duration. Applying for scholarships is highly recommended, as you might be successful.

Visa Costs

It is best to consult a counselor regarding the student visa process, as it must not be fiddled with. A valid student visa comes with its costs and can cost an application fee of USD 160.

Accommodation Costs

Opting for on-campus accommodation is generally preferable for students, especially international ones. It tends to be more affordable and facilitates easier connection with peers, which can be beneficial for your educational needs. Living among both international and local students in similar programs can enhance your social life, provide convenient academic support, and help you adjust more easily to a new country. It's an effective way to build friendships quickly.

The main challenge is that on-campus housing may not be available to everyone, often allocated based on academic merit or a first-come-first-served system. Therefore, booking a spot as early as possible is crucial.

Students who prefer off-campus living commonly rent apartments with roommates (often from the same university or background) or choose a homestay with a local family. Universities typically offer assistance to students in finding both on-campus and off-campus housing. Accommodation costs vary by location, but students should budget approximately US $6,000 to $14,000 annually for housing.

Living Expenses

Living expenses cover a variety of sub-categories but essentially refer to all things you need to survive in a city, such as food, transportation, toiletries, social activities, etc. It is a good practice to set a budget beforehand and document each expense so as not to overspend.

Considering all costs, a student budget for one lies between US $10,000 to $20,000 each academic year. A comprehensive breakdown of the list of expenses per month is as follows:

Food and Drinks	($2500)
Clothing	($500)
Books and Stationery	($500 – $1,000)
Transport	($500 – $1200)
Other	($2,000)

Test Requirements

The SAT is a widely recognized standardized test for college admissions in the United States, assessing reading, writing, and math comprehension to demonstrate a student's knowledge and application skills.

The GRE (Graduate Record Examinations) serves as an alternative, required by many graduate schools in the U.S., Canada, and some other countries. It evaluates verbal reasoning, quantitative reasoning, critical thinking, and analytical writing abilities.

Sports Scholarships

University sports in America are at the highest level in the world, so universities carefully select promising candidates for their sports teams and, even more carefully, those whose education and training they will fund.

Athletes who are trained in the US universities will receive the following:

- Condensed for time, but a complete knowledge, a training program.

- A minimum of 20 hours of training per week.

- Individual study schedules are based on the training and competition plans.

- Training with the best coaches and regular participation in competitions.

- To qualify for a sports scholarship, you must:

- Have outstanding sports results.

- Know English at the level corresponding to the admission requirements of the University.

- Pass the SAT/ACT/GRE subject tests at the entrance requirements level.

- Have the grades, i.e., GPA, at the entrance requirements level.

- Demonstrate discipline, high motivation, and excellent knowledge of the sport.

Chapter 5

~Studying in Canada

Canada is one of the best places to study abroad. You would want to go to Canada for many reasons.

Canada is often recognized for its high quality of life. In 2022, the U.S. News & World Report ranked Canada third globally for quality of life. The country is known for respecting human rights, diversity, equality, stability, and peace, and international students generally have the same rights and freedoms as Canadian citizens.

Canada provides flexible and high-quality education and research opportunities across various levels. Students can often transfer between different educational types and levels more easily compared to some other countries. There are over 8,000 colleges and 16,000 university programs available, with approximately seven Canadian universities ranking among the top 200 globally.

Canada is considered a welcoming, safe, and culturally diverse nation, with communities and classrooms that aim to make people feel at home. The country is home to over 250 ethnic origins and 200 languages from around the world, including nearly 70 indigenous languages.

Compared to countries like Australia, the U.K., and the U.S., Canada often offers more affordable and accessible scholarships and work opportunities for international students to help finance their education. Many programs include work placements or internships for practical experience. Most international students are eligible to work while studying and can apply for a post-graduate work permit after completing their studies. Tuition fees are also generally lower than in the aforementioned countries.

Apart from the environment and affordable education, Canada is home to some of the top universities in the world!

1. University of Toronto

The top university in Canada is the University of Toronto, ranking 25th worldwide. The university climbed four places in this year's rankings and earned high scores across most indicators, especially in terms of academic reputation, where it ranks 15th worldwide.

2. McGill University

McGill University is in Montreal and remains in second place in Canada this year. It rose four spots in the rankings to 31st place. McGill University produced 12 Nobel laureates and 145 Rhodes Scholars among its alums and Canada's current prime minister, Justin Trudeau.

3. University of British Columbia

One of the top three universities in the country is the University of British Columbia, which ranks third in Canada and 45th in the whole world. It rose six places this year. Now, it ranks 28th in the world for the academic reputation indicator. The University of British Columbia embraces innovation and challenges the status quo.

4. Université de Montréal

Université de Montréal ranks fourth among Canada's top universities. It is a French-language public research university in Montreal, founded in 1878, and it has over 67,350 students, including 10,000 international students.

5. University of Alberta

The University of Alberta holds the 119th spot. It welcomes 40,000 students across its four campuses. Its highest score comes from the international faculty indicator.

Once you've chosen a university in Canada, it's crucial to review the eligibility criteria and admission requirements. Verify if the institution is a Designated Learning Institution (DLI) to ensure it's recognized by Canada and to avoid educational scams.

Tuition fees are a significant factor in your study expenses. These costs vary depending on the country and the specific academic program. Universities typically provide detailed tuition information for each program on their websites. Additionally, research the language of instruction, as Canada is bilingual, offering Master's degrees in English, French, or both.

Strong academic grades are vital for your application. Many Canadian institutions require an average score of 70% or higher. A higher percentage generally increases your chances of enrolling in a prestigious university. If you are over 25 and graduated from your last program at least two years prior to applying, you'll likely need to provide details about your previous employment history.

Given the availability of Master's degrees taught in both English and French, students must demonstrate their language proficiency through recognized tests. The primary English language tests accepted by top Canadian universities include:

- IELTS Academic

- PTE Academic

- C1 Advanced

- TOEFL iBT

- Some universities also accept other English tests, like:

- CAEL (Canadian Academic English Language Assessment)

- CanTEST (Canadian Test of English for Scholars and Trainees)

- MELAB (Michigan English Language Assessment Battery)

- French tests accepted by universities in Canada

- DALF

- DELF

- TEF

- TCF

You must also be careful while picking the study program of your choice. This can be tricky because Canadian universities offer many different types of programs with unique features. However, there are certain things to look out for during this process.

Are scholarships available?

This is perhaps one of the most important factors when choosing a study program. There are many scholarship opportunities available to international students in Canada. If this is a priority, make sure to check out what your prospective department or program is offering.

How does a Canadian study program help your overall career goals?

When you have a clear idea of your future career goals, you can focus on programs that can assist you in getting there. You can look through university and college course listings and read their detailed descriptions to understand what's covered in a program.

Is this program compatible with your life right now?

Most international students in Canada bring their families along with them, or they have work commitments during their studying years. Finding a study program that fits your current lifestyle is the key to finding the perfect program that caters to your needs.

Luckily, Canada offers a multitude of financial aid and scholarship programs!

1. Banting Postdoctoral Fellowships

This prestigious CAD 70,000 annual scholarship, awarded for two years, aims to attract top-tier national and international postgraduate students.

2. IDRC Research Awards

This scholarship opportunity is available to students from developing countries, providing a financial sum disbursed throughout the duration of their academic program.

3. Vanier Canada Graduate Scholarships Program

The Canadian government provides a generous scholarship of CAD 50,000 annually for up to three years to Master's students in fields such as Science, Engineering, and Humanities.

4. Shastri Indo-Canadian Institute

These fellowships support various graduate and postgraduate Indian students enrolled at esteemed universities, enabling eligible individuals to access courses or online coaching from any Canadian university under the SICI program.

5. Canadian Commonwealth Scholarship and Fellowship Plan

Students hailing from the commonwealth nations can avail of several grants every year. This scholarship changes every year to provide different privileges.

6. Ontario Graduate Scholarship Program

The Ontario scholarship provides grants to students who enroll in Ontario public universities. You can get from 5000 CAD - 15 000 CAD.

7. Ontario Trillium Scholarship

This scholarship awards international PhD students up to CAD 40,000 over a period of four years.

8. Canada-ASEAN SEED

Global Affairs Canada offers scholarships for higher studies that cover expenses such as visa/study/work permit fees, airfare, health insurance, living costs, ground transportation, books, and supplies.

9. Quebec Provincial Government Scholarship

Financial assistance for students in Quebec, currently paused, previously offered scholarships up to CAD 40,000. The National Research Council of Canada (NRCC) provides research grants to Master's and PhD research students, with the amount and duration varying based on the level of study.

The best part about studying in Canada is that you don't only enjoy the accessible and affordable higher education opportunities but also enjoy post-graduate job opportunities in the country! To work in Canada after you graduate, you need a work permit. The work experience you gain while working may help you qualify for permanent residence.

Post-graduation work permit (PGWP)

Graduates of certain designated learning institutions are eligible for this work permit.

Canadian Experience Class

The Canadian Experience Class (CEC) program, managed through the Express Entry immigration system, offers a swift pathway to Canadian permanent residence for those who meet specific eligibility criteria, including age, language proficiency, education level, and, crucially, at least 12 months of continuous, full-time skilled work experience in Canada within the last three years (or an equivalent in part-time experience), making it a potentially ideal immigration option for eligible international students after graduation.

Federal Skilled Worker Program

The Federal Skilled Worker (FSW) program, also managed through the Express Entry system, presents another avenue for permanent residency for international student graduates. Unlike the Canadian Experience Class (CEC), the FSW program does not necessitate Canadian work experience, making it suitable for graduates who have already accumulated skilled work experience internationally. This merit-based program uses a points system called the Comprehensive Ranking System (CRS) to evaluate and rank applicants, inviting only the highest-scoring candidates to apply for permanent residence. If an international student meets the eligibility criteria, including a minimum of 12 months of continuous, full-time skilled work experience (or its part-time equivalent, gained either in Canada or abroad), and scores competitively within the CRS, the FSW can be a viable pathway to permanent residency, though it's not an option for those without prior workforce experience.

Provincial Nominee Programs

Each of Canada's provinces and territories has its own unique immigration programs. These are called Provincial Nominee Programs (PNPs). Every PNP has a different way of working and structuring to meet the needs of that specific province or territory. Many PNPs offer preference to applicants with a link to the province, including previous study programs completed within the region and work experience gained there. International students may be eligible to apply for a PNP within a province, depending on the area where they completed their study program.

Important facts to know before you apply

- Months for academic Intakes fall in the fall (September), winter (January), and summer (May.)

- There are a total of 223 universities in Canada, and collectively, they house more than 750,000 international students.

- The average tuition fee is CAD 18,000 per annum, and the average cost of living is CAD 10,000 per annum.

Student Life

Opting for a Canadian university for higher education immerses you in a vibrant country that warmly welcomes over 750,000 international students, offering a rich tapestry of cultural diversity and countless opportunities to enjoy life. As a student, you'll forge new friendships and explore diverse cultures and languages through team projects, campus socializing, and sports, potentially even experiencing ice hockey or baseball. Exciting experiences abound, from dining and performances in major cities like Toronto, Montreal, Vancouver, Ottawa, and Calgary to ice skating on the Rideau Canal or exploring Banff National Park's stunning landscapes. Navigating daily life, balancing studies, work, and personal responsibilities, will foster personal growth and make you a source of pride for yourself and your family.

Once in Canada, don't forget to register with your country's embassy or consulate office.

Visa Process

1. Study Permit

This is for students who want to study in Canada for over six months. You should apply for a study permit when you receive your acceptance letter from a designated learning institution. In this way, you can arrive in Canada up to four weeks before the start of your program.

2. Student Partnership Program (SPP) visa

The Student Direct Stream (SDS) visa is for students from specific countries intending to study in Canada for over six months, and the optimal application time is after receiving acceptance from a participating Canadian educational institution, allowing arrival up to four weeks before program commencement. Canada has become a leading global destination for higher education, particularly for students from developing nations, attracting students from over 100 countries for nearly a decade and a half. Indian students currently comprise the largest group of international students in Canada (34%) with a 21% annual growth rate and have been the top recipients of Canadian Permanent Residence since 2017.

Canada boasts advanced educational infrastructure and top instructors, ensuring high-quality academic outcomes and a wide variety of credentials at its universities and government colleges.

Choosing Canada for higher studies provides access to excellent resources and inclusive programs; explore the top universities to find the best fit for your finances, grades, lifestyle, and career goals, and remember to apply for available scholarships. Importantly, pursuing education in Canada offers a pathway to potentially settling permanently in a beautiful country renowned for its human rights advocacy.

Chapter 6

Studying in the UK

Students globally are drawn to study in the UK for its esteemed education, diverse culture, and vibrant student cities, creating an appealing environment for international study. Recent UK initiatives, such as visa adjustments and more flexible immigration policies, aim to attract even more international students, with a goal of 600,000 annually by 2030; between 2019 and 2020, international students constituted roughly 22% of the university population. UK universities are particularly renowned for their medicine, arts, and humanities programs, offering over 100 institutions for international students.

The UK's significant diversity, with approximately 14% of its population born abroad (around 9.5 million people), allows international students to immerse themselves in various cultures and build a global network of friends. A key benefit of studying in the UK is the abundance of career opportunities, especially in fields listed on the UK's Shortage Occupation List, such as nursing, pharmacy, teaching, and engineering, for which the government actively seeks international professionals.

The list of the world's top universities that reside in the UK is almost endless, but the following ones are the most known and sought after:

University of Oxford

Retaking first place in the UK this year is the University of Oxford, which drops one place in the global rankings to fifth. Achieving high scores across all indicators, Oxford is the highest-ranked school in the UK for faculty-student ratio (eighth place) and citations per faculty (44th place).

University of Cambridge

Cambridge is in second place and ranked seventh globally. However, Cambridge is the highest-ranked university in the UK for academic and employer reputation, in second place globally for these indicators.

Imperial College London

Taking the bronze medal position in the UK is Imperial College London, the highest-ranked university in the capital. It moves up one position globally this year to eighth place and ranks ninth for academic reputation.

UCL (University College London)

UCL ranks 10th globally, and its highest score can be found in the academic reputation indicator, where it places 13th in the world.

University of Edinburgh

Ranking fifth in the UK and remaining the 20th best university in the world is the University of Edinburgh – the only Scottish institution in the UK top 10. It scores particularly highly for academic and employer reputations, ranking 25th and 31st in the world, respectively, for these indicators.

The University of Manchester

The University of Manchester ranks sixth in the UK this year, taking joint 27th place in the global rankings. Employers look at Manchester graduates particularly favorably – the university ranks 21st in the world for the employer reputation indicator.

King's College London (KCL)

Seventh in the UK again this year is King's College London (KCL), which climbed two places in the global rankings to joint 31st. One of four London-based universities in the UK's top 10, KCL achieves impressive scores in all indicators, particularly academic reputation, where it ranks among the top 50 universities worldwide.

Students globally are drawn to study in the UK for its esteemed education, diverse culture, and vibrant student cities, creating an appealing environment for international study. Recent UK initiatives, such as visa adjustments and more flexible immigration policies, aim to attract even more international students, with a goal of 600,000 annually by 2030; between 2019 and 2020, international students constituted roughly 22% of the university population. UK universities are particularly renowned for their medicine, arts, and humanities programs, offering over 100 institutions for international students. The UK's significant diversity, with approximately 14% of its population born abroad (around 9.5 million people), allows international students to immerse themselves in various cultures and build a global network of friends. A key benefit of studying in the UK is the abundance of career opportunities, especially in fields listed on the UK's Shortage Occupation List, such as nursing, pharmacy, teaching, and engineering, for which the government actively seeks international professionals.

Requirements to study in the UK at the undergraduate level:

- Certificate for completing 10+2 education from a recognized Indian board with minimum marks.

- Original academic transcripts from previous institutions.

- Statement of Purpose

- Letters of Recommendations

- Scores of English Proficiency Tests

- Passport and other ID proof

- Bank statements to provide evidence of Financial Funds

- Offer Letter

- Student visa

Chevening Scholarships

The UK government's Chevening Scholarships are prestigious global awards for outstanding scholars from eligible countries, typically for a one-year Master's degree. These scholarships usually cover tuition, a living allowance, return airfare and essential grants.

Scotland Saltire Scholarships

The Scottish Government, in partnership with Scottish universities, offers Scotland's Saltire Scholarships to citizens from Canada, China (including Hong Kong), India, Japan, Pakistan, and the USA for full-time Master's degrees in science, technology, creative industries, healthcare and medical sciences, and renewable and clean energy. Each scholarship provides £8,000 towards tuition for one year.

Commonwealth Masters Scholarships

Commonwealth Scholarships support students from developing Commonwealth countries pursuing Master's studies in the UK. Funded by the UK Department for International Development (DFID), these scholarships include airfare, tuition and examination fees, a personal maintenance allowance, a thesis grant (if applicable), and an initial arrival allowance.

GREAT scholarships

A GREAT scholarship offers £10,000 towards tuition for a one-year Master's program in the UK. This is a partnership between the British Government and participating universities. Eligibility is limited to 14 countries, and applicants should check their university's funding page for availability and application instructions.

Simmons University Kotzen Scholarships

Simmons University Kotzen Scholarships are fully funded undergraduate scholarships for international students, covering full tuition, mandatory fees, and room and board.

Imperial College London PhD Scholarship

The Imperial College London Ph.D. Scholarship is a fully funded program for international students. Up to 10 scholarships are awarded annually, covering tuition fees and providing a tax-free annual maintenance allowance of £16,553.

Preparing for Your Student Visa Application

Once you have identified the scholarship program that best suits you, the next step is to ensure you meet all visa requirements. To avoid confusion, it is helpful to have a detailed checklist.

Essential Documents for Your Visa Application

1. A Valid Passport or Travel Document

   o   Ensure your passport is current and valid for travel.

2. Confirmation of Acceptance for Studies (CAS) Requirements

   o   You must disclose the qualifications listed in your CAS (Confirmation of Acceptance for Studies).

   o   If no qualifications are listed in your CAS, you are not required to provide any additional documents.

3. Proof of English Language Proficiency

   o   Universities determine how they assess a student's English language skills.

   o   Your CAS will confirm the method of assessment. If a certificate or qualification is required, it will be listed in your CAS, and you must provide the corresponding document.

   o   If no English language qualifications are listed in your CAS, you do not need to submit any additional proof.

4. Translations of Non-English Documents

   o   If any document is not in English, it must be accompanied by a complete and certified translation that includes:

   o   A statement from the translator confirming the accuracy of the translation.

   o   The translation company's contact details.

   o   The date of translation.

5. Proof of Financial Support

- o You must provide evidence that you have sufficient funds to cover tuition fees and living expenses in the UK.

- o Refer to official financial guidelines to determine the required amount.

Acceptable financial documents include:

- o Personal bank statements or building society statements

- o Bank letters

- o Official loan letters

- o Official financial sponsorship letters

By carefully preparing these documents, you can streamline your visa application process and avoid unnecessary delays.

You must provide a letter of consent from any government sponsor if you've received official financial sponsorship in the past year, confirming their approval for your Student Visa application. Additionally, some postgraduate students require an ATAS (Academic Technology Approval Scheme) certificate, which can take about a month to process; your CAS will confirm if this is needed.

Despite the checklist, the benefits of a UK education are significant, especially considering the diverse work visas available to international students. Five work visa options exist:

The Tier 2 (General) visa, the most common route for international students seeking UK employment post-studies, addresses labor market shortages. Applicants need a minimum salary of £21,000+ per year, and their employer must be a licensed Tier 2 sponsor.

The Tier 4 Doctorate Extension Scheme allows PhD graduates an extra 12 months in the UK to seek employment, gain experience, or start a business.

The Tier 5 (Youth Mobility Scheme) visa offers young adults from Australia, Canada, Hong Kong, Japan, Monaco, New Zealand, the Republic of Korea, or Taiwan the chance to work in the UK for up to two years post-graduation. Places are limited, and applications cannot be made from within the UK.

A start-up visa supports international graduates with innovative and scalable business ideas in the UK. It requires an endorsement letter from a UK university or a recognized business organization.

Securing a work permit is the initial step towards a wealth of promising job opportunities that can shape your future. While a Tier 4 student visa is needed for study, a Tier 2 (general) work visa is required for eligible employment with an approved employer. For those starting a business, a Tier 1 visa is necessary. This initial five-year work permit offers a significant period to build your future and plan for permanent settlement in the UK.

The UK job market welcomes skilled international graduates. Prominent industries offering opportunities include:

Engineering: The UK boasts advanced engineering education with extensive research and practical training, preparing graduates for the job market.

Healthcare: With a renowned healthcare system, the UK has a consistent demand for healthcare professionals, offering rewarding careers with competitive salaries. This field requires dedication due to the intensity of its programs.

Accountancy and Finance: Professionals in accountancy and finance are essential for all companies, leading to high demand and numerous job opportunities for international students across the UK.

Marketing and Sales: While competition can be strong, the marketing and sales sector offers significant scope for growth, financial rewards, and job satisfaction for those who succeed.

Overall, the UK is a prime destination for international students seeking education and subsequent employment, provided they navigate the visa process and leverage available scholarship opportunities.

Chapter 7

Studying in Australia

Australia stands out as a top choice for higher education, offering strong academics, a high standard of living, and significant support for international students across various fields like MBA, engineering, humanities, and English language courses.

The quality of life in Australia is ranked second globally, featuring sophisticated infrastructure, excellent healthcare, diverse public transport, numerous student services, and a relatively affordable cost of living. It's a major hub for international study, boasting five of the world's top 30 student cities based on quality of life, job prospects, cost of living, and student community.

The Australian Government provides substantial incentives for international students, including around $200 million in scholarships, job visas in various sectors, research opportunities, and pathways to permanent residency after graduation. The Tertiary Education Quality and Standards Agency (TEQSA) ensures quality and monitors higher education providers through established standards. The Education Services for Overseas Students (ESOS) law protects the well-being of international students, the quality of their academic experience, and the provision of accurate information.

Australia offers a wide array of well-regarded and internationally recognized universities. In the 2021 QS World University Rankings, 36 Australian universities were listed, with most showing improvement in their rankings. Some of the top universities in Australia include:

Australian National University (ANU)

Australian National University (ANU) is the top Australian university, scoring well across almost all indicators, including academic reputation, international faculty, international students, and citations per faculty ratio indicators, ranking within the top 50 worldwide.

University of Sydney

The University of Sydney is Australia's second-best university, and it rose two places this year, ranking 40th worldwide. It has perfect scores in the international faculty and international students' indicators. The University of Sydney was Australia's first university and is a member of the Group of Eight. It was established in 1850.

University of Melbourne

The University of Melbourne stands proud as the 41st top university in the world. It shines as the top-ranked university in Australia, earning high praise from academics and employers. Globally, it holds a strong position, landing 30th place out of 283 universities and making it into the top 30 list for its notable reputation. The university also ranks well in the international students' indicator, and international students make up 42% of its student population, arriving from more than 130 countries.

University of New South Wales (UNSW)

In 44th place is the University of New South Wales (UNSW). It remains in fourth place in Australia. UNSW is a founding member of the Group of Eight, a group of Australian research-based universities. The university places in the top 50 for all but one of the indicators.

University of Queensland (UQ)

The university's alumni include two Nobel laureates, Peter C. Dogerty and John Harsanyi; Academy Award winner Geoffrey Rush; and leaders in government, law, science, public service, and the arts. Researchers from UQ have been responsible for several recent innovations, such as the cervical cancer vaccine.

Monash University

It ranks among the world's 50 best universities for its academic reputation indicator and holds a perfect score in the international students' indicator. Monash University is located in Melbourne and has five campuses in the state of Victoria and two overseas, in Malaysia and South Africa.

University of Western Australia (UWA)

UWA beats all Australian universities above it for the proportion of international faculty members and the number of citations per faculty member, which measures research output).

University of Adelaide

The University of Adelaide was established in 1874, and it is Australia's third oldest university, placing 106th place in this year in the world university rankings. The University of Adelaide ranks 44th worldwide for the international students indicator, and more than 7,860 of the university's 21,142 students are international students from over 100 different countries.

University of Technology Sydney (UTS)

UTS scores exceptionally well in the citations per faculty, international students, and employer reputation indicators, ranking 67th, 78th, and 85th, respectively. UTS is one of the youngest top Australian universities. They aim to advance knowledge through research-inspired teaching, using their partnerships with industry, professions, and the community.

University of Wollongong

This university performs well for the citations per faculty indicator, ranking 75th globally. The University of Wollongong was founded initially in 1975, with donations from local people. The university has partnered with its communities to make an impact in the Illawarra region and address society's economic, environmental, social, and medical challenges.

Entry Requirements:

Undergraduate Program

The candidate should have finished 12 years of schooling, matching the level of Australian qualification standards. They need to score at least 60% in four subjects to pass. They must get their degree from a recognized school.

Postgraduate (Masters) program:

Bachelor's degree attained from a recognized institute. The bachelor's degree must be equivalent to an Australian bachelor's degree deemed by qualification assessment references from your selected university. Minimum grades acquired in subjects require knowledge and working experience, depending on the study program you have selected for admission.

Postgraduate (PhD) program:

Master's degree or Bachelor's honors degree must be equivalent to Australian qualification assessment references of your selected Australian University. The program you choose will determine the grades you need, the skills you must have, any research work required, the work experience you should possess, and the academic ability you need to show.

Language Requirements:

Australia is an English-speaking country; therefore, you will mostly find English-taught programs to study there at all academic levels. In countries where English is not a native language, students need to fulfill English proficiency requirements by passing one of the English language proficiency tests. IELTS course is accepted for admissions and student visas in Australia. Apart from IELTS, students can also do the following English language proficiency tests for admission to Australian Universities:

- Cambridge Advanced English (CAE),

- Pearson Test of English (PTE) Academic module,

- TOEFL Internet based Test (iBT)

The minimum grades and scores can be ascertained by Australian Universities for admission requirements. The minimum passing score for IELTS must be 6.0, with a writing grade of 5.5. Australian universities will only accept band scores of 5.0 or higher.

Documents Required for Admissions:

Australian universities accept admission applications directly submitted at their official website. The student must present an online application form and a PDF file of the required documents. The submission requirement may vary from one Australian university to another and according to the study program:

- Paid admission fee receipt

- Filled application form

- English language proficiency test certificate

- Copy of passport and national identity card

- Statement of intent, explaining why the applicant has chosen a specific study program for admissions

- Bank statement to prove that the person can afford tuition fees and living expenses

- Work experience, particularly in post-graduate courses

- Recommendation letters, which are written by the applicant's teacher stating the applicant's academic eligibility

Choosing the right program:

Ultimately, your future aspirations should guide your choice of study. Select a field that builds upon your previous education and aligns with your career goals, offering both personal and professional growth. Consider the employability prospects after graduation and whether you plan to stay in Australia or return home, as this will influence your program selection.

Compile a list of suitable courses and research them along with the institutions offering them, utilizing information available on college websites. Evaluate the gathered details to determine the best option for your individual needs.

The duration of your program directly affects your stay in Australia, with longer programs typically offering more extended post-study work options and influencing the validity of your student visa.

Tuition costs are a crucial factor. Clarify whether the advertised price is per semester, year, or for the entire program to effectively manage your budget.

Researching potential cities is also important. Developed areas often provide more job opportunities and better public transport but come with higher accommodation costs. Consider whether an urban or suburban environment suits your preferences.

Funding is a significant consideration. Explore the various scholarships Australia offers to international students, which can cover expenses ranging from tuition fees to accommodation.

Australia Awards

The Australia Awards aim to foster educational connections and lasting relationships between Australia and its neighboring countries through its comprehensive scholarship programs, uniting scholarships from the Department of Foreign Affairs (DFAT), the Department of Education, and the Australian Centre for International Agricultural Research (ACIAR).

Destination Australia:

The Destination Australia Program (DAP), an Australian Government initiative, provides funding to eligible tertiary institutions to offer scholarships to both domestic and international students for studying in regional Australia. These scholarships are valued at up to $15,000 per student annually and support studies from Certificate IV to Ph.D. levels for up to four years at regional campuses throughout Australia.

Learn more about the Research Training Program at the Department of Education website. Applications for these scholarships are made directly to a participating university.

Provider scholarships:

Australian education providers regularly offer scholarships to qualifying international students based on academic merit. Consult with the admissions team or international office at the provider you are applying to for further advice and information.

Application Process:

Applying to high-ranking Australian universities involves a standardized, though potentially detailed, process. A checklist simplifies this:

- Completed Application Form.

- TOEFL/IELTS/PTE Exam Score (to demonstrate English proficiency).

- Academic Certificates (SSC, Inter, Bachelor's degrees and transcripts).

- Photocopies of passport (first and last pages).

- Job Experience Certificates (if applicable).

- Medium of Instruction (MOI) certificate.

- Any Other Specified Documents.

For admission, English language proficiency tests like TOEFL, IELTS, or PTE are required for most courses, especially Master's and business programs, to assess the candidate's ability to succeed.

Academic qualifications must be supported by official certificates and transcripts. For undergraduate applications, SSC and higher secondary certificates are needed. For postgraduate applications, bachelor's and/or master's degree certificates and mark sheets are required. Specific documents include 10th and 12th-grade transcripts and certificates, bachelor's and master's transcripts and degrees (if applicable), diploma transcripts and certificates (if applicable), and any additional diplomas or certificates.

Experience in a relevant field is often necessary for business program admissions but not for undergraduate courses. Experience certificates can strengthen postgraduate applications and include the latest joining letter, latest salary slip, employment certificates from previous employers, and an experience letter.

Many international students in Australia aspire to permanent residency. However, General Skilled Migration rules are subject to change, making it an uncertain path without guarantees. The typical initial step is obtaining a post-study work visa, followed by an application for General Skilled Migration for Permanent Residency (PR). While the process can be lengthy and complex, Australia offers numerous high-paying job opportunities in diverse fields, particularly for postgraduate international students, making the pursuit worthwhile.

Chapter 8

Studying in Singapore

Studying abroad offers enriching experiences and a competitive educational edge. Singapore stands out as an excellent and surprisingly affordable destination for American students. Many programs offer international student scholarships and grants, and the cost of living is lower than in the US, UK, and Australia.

Beyond affordability, Singapore is a culturally rich and diverse country attracting students globally. Its universities foster networking opportunities with students from China, Malaysia, India, Europe, and beyond. Singapore's harmonious society values cultural diversity, with significant Hindu, Buddhist, Christian, and Muslim populations, allowing students to explore various religious sites and deepen their cultural understanding.

Since its independence in 1965, Singapore's economy has grown significantly, becoming a leading hub for aerospace, engineering, IT, pharmaceuticals, biotechnology, and other industries. The presence of numerous multinational company headquarters provides students with valuable connections to potential employers.

Overall, studying in Singapore offers a world-class education within a diverse and welcoming culture. Its affordable costs, strong economy, and growing industries make it a compelling choice for American students seeking to broaden their perspectives and enhance their academic and career prospects.

Here are some of the top universities in Singapore.

1. National University of Singapore

The National University of Singapore (NUS), the oldest higher education institution in the country, offers a wide range of degree programs across three campuses and 16 faculties. With over 370 degrees available, including bachelor's, master's, doctoral degrees, and graduate diplomas, students have plenty of options. NUS is also home to a diverse community of students and staff from over 100 countries, creating a multicultural environment.

2. Nanyang Technological University, Singapore

Established in 1981, Nanyang Technological University, Singapore (NTU) is a well-regarded public university that focuses on research across various fields, including engineering, business, humanities, arts and social sciences, and medicine. To enhance its offerings, the university collaborates with prestigious international partners like Imperial College London to provide exceptional education to its undergraduate and graduate students. As part of this partnership, NTU has opened a new medical school to ensure its students receive the best education and training.

3. Singapore University of Technology and Design

Singapore University of Technology and Design is a renowned institution in Singapore that students worldwide are highly sought after. The university acknowledges the crucial role that arts and design play in technological and societal advancements, a fact that has been overlooked for a long time. It recognizes that these aspects are equally important as the more technical and scientific areas of study, which sets it apart from other institutions.

4. Singapore Management University

When considering a study abroad opportunity in Singapore, having multiple options is important. One highly regarded choice is Singapore Management University (SMU). Established in 2000, SMU is an independent academic institution that offers degree programs in business and computer fields and is recognized as one of the top universities in Asia. It has a diverse student population of over 12,600, with over 10% of students coming from other countries.

5. INSEAD Asia Campus

INSEAD Asia Campus is a highly-regarded institution for international students seeking higher education in Singapore. The private business school, which originated in France and is known as Institut Européen d'Administration des Affaires, has expanded its reach with a campus in Singapore since 1999. The campus offers graduate degree programs in various fields, allowing students in Asia to pursue their studies without the need to travel to the main campus in Europe. With excellent programs and facilities, INSEAD Asia Campus is a top choice for those seeking a high-quality education in Singapore.

6. Singapore University of Social Sciences

In addition to academic and research excellence, it is vital to take into account extracurricular activities, leadership involvement, and future career prospects when deciding on a university to attend. Singapore University of Social Sciences is a top-notch institution that excels in these areas, making it an ideal choice for prospective students.

7. Singapore Institute of Technology

For those aiming for swift entry into the workforce, the Singapore Institute of Technology is the ideal destination. The institution is a specialized university concentrating on practical education to create skilled professionals who contribute significantly to society's development and economic growth. SIT's degree programs are tailored to match the current requirements of different industries, guaranteeing students quality education relevant to the world of work. Engineering and business courses are among the programs provided by the university to meet society's needs, and SIT strives to satisfy this need by delivering high-quality education.

8. Nanyang Academy of Fine Arts

Nanyang Academy of Fine Arts (NAFA) is a certified higher education institution in Singapore that provides focused learning programs in Fine Arts, Design, and Music. The university offers both diploma and bachelor's degree courses to students.

9. LASALLE College of the Arts

With a mission to groom innovative and visionary artists, designers, and leaders of creative industries, LASALLE College of the Arts stands out as one of the top schools for art and design in Asia. The college offers a diverse range of undergraduate and graduate programs across various fields, including fine arts, design, media arts, and performing arts. With a strong commitment to nurturing creative talent and fostering a vibrant arts community, LASALLE has become a premier institution in Singapore, attracting students from all over the world who are passionate about pursuing a career in the arts.

10. Singapore Aviation Academy

Established in 1958, the Singapore Aviation Academy is a renowned aviation school that provides international standard training programs in aviation. As the training arm of the Civil Aviation Authority of Singapore, it offers diploma, bachelor's, and master's degree programs to equip aspiring professionals with the skills and knowledge necessary to meet the demands of the global aviation industry. The academy strives to cultivate the next generation of experts who can lead and contribute to the aviation field, and it has earned a reputation for excellence in aviation education.

Entry requirements:

Language Proficiency Requirement

In Singaporean universities, showing a good grasp of English is important. Students need to take certain tests to prove their language skills. These tests, like IELTS, TOEFL, and PTE, are a must to meet the entry requirements.

IELTS

To be eligible for undergraduate and graduate programs, a globally recognized English proficiency test, IELTS, is required, with a recommended score range of 6 to 6.5 for admission to reputable universities.

TOEFL

Even though TOEFL scores are commonly used for admission to universities in North America, many universities in Singapore also use them to assess language proficiency. The minimum score required for the internet-based test is 100 or above, valid for two years.

PTE Academic

Instead of IELTS and TOEFL, PTE Academic is also an acceptable language proficiency test for students who wish to study in a foreign university. It is a computer-based exam with an average score of 68 that is required for admission.

The following 10 universities in Singapore accept PTE:

- National University of Singapore

- Nanyang Technological University

- PSB Academy

- INSEAD

- East Asia Institute of Management

- Dimensions International College

- Leadership and Management Institute

- Curtin University

- London School of Business and Finance, Singapore

- Heart power Tesol and Teacher Training Centre

SAT (Scholarship Aptitude Test)

This is a standardized test taken by high school students who wish to enroll in an undergraduate program. It assesses their skills in reading, writing, and mathematics.

How can you pick the right program?

Choosing a university program necessitates careful consideration of your interests, as they significantly impact your enjoyment of university life and can guide you toward suitable courses. Additionally, evaluate the importance of co-op or internship opportunities. While beneficial for gaining work experience and career insights, co-op programs may reduce leisure time, so align this option with your priorities.

Most universities offer hands-on learning experiences like labs, field trips, student teams, study abroad, co-ops, internships, and studio courses. These experiential opportunities enhance understanding by applying concepts practically and are particularly valuable for kinesthetic learners. When researching universities, prioritize those that offer your preferred balance of traditional classroom learning and experiential activities.

Beyond academics, extracurricular activities such as residence life, sports, clubs, student government, and volunteering are crucial for a well-rounded university experience. They provide avenues for socialization, relationship building, and skill development outside the classroom. When selecting a university, consider the availability of activities that align with your interests, whether it's specific sports or a wide range of options.

In essence, selecting the right university program involves a thoughtful assessment of your interests, the value you place on co-op or internships, the availability of experiential learning, and the range of extracurricular activities offered. By considering these elements, you can identify a program that aligns with your academic and personal goals, equips you with the necessary skills, and ensures a fulfilling university experience.

Scholarship options for funding:

Singapore International Graduate Award (SINGA)

The ASTAR Joint International PhD Scholarship is a collaborative scholarship offered by ASTAR, NUS, NTU, and SMU in Singapore. It provides international students pursuing a PhD in science, engineering, and technology with full tuition fee coverage, a monthly stipend, and other allowances.

President's Graduate Fellowship (PGF)

International students interested in pursuing a PhD in any field of study offered by the National University of Singapore (NUS) and the Nanyang Technological University (NTU) can apply for this scholarship. It is available exclusively to international students and offers financial support covering tuition fees, monthly stipends, and other allowances.

Monbukagakusho Research Scholarship (MEXT)

The Japanese government provides a scholarship for international students wanting to undertake graduate-level research studies in Japan. Singaporean and Singapore Permanent Residents are also eligible to apply for this scholarship.

Lee Kuan Yew Global Business Plan Competition Scholarships

The LKY-SMILE scholarship program was created in collaboration with the LKY School of Public Policy by the Singapore Management University Institute of Innovation and Entrepreneurship.

ISCA-ICAI International Scholarships

International students interested in studying accountancy in Singapore can apply for a scholarship offered jointly by the Institute of Singapore Chartered Accountants (ISCA) and the Institute of Chartered Accountants of India (ICAI).

Documents required for a Singaporean student visa:

- Passport (Original & photocopy)

- Proof of funds

- Bank statements

- Application form

- Academic mark sheets

- Medical reports

- Visa application fees

- Letter of acceptance from a Singaporean university

Permanent residency (PR)/ Citizenship options:

Foreign Students Scheme

One way international students studying in Singapore can apply for permanent residence (PR) is by showcasing exceptional academic performance. However, they must have:

- resided in Singapore for more than two years

- passed any national exam like GCE 'N'/'O'/'A' levels or PSLE or are enrolled in the Integrated Program (IP).

Work Pass

Students who have completed their higher education at Singaporean universities can apply for permanent residency if they secure employment there. To be eligible for full-time work in Singapore, these graduates must obtain one of the following passes.

- Employment- passes for qualified professionals and graduates

- S -Passes for skilled foreign workers employed in Singapore.

Foreign nationals seeking permanent residency in Singapore must apply through the electronic Permanent Residence (e-PR) system. To legally work in Singapore, non-residents must first obtain a work pass, which is facilitated by their employer upon securing a job.

However, a work pass is employer-specific, meaning it is valid only for the sponsoring employer. If an individual changes jobs, their current work pass is revoked, and their new employer must apply for a new one.

Types of Work Passes in Singapore

Applicants can apply for one of two work passes, depending on their **salary and qualifications**:

- **S Pass** – Typically issued to fresh graduates and mid-level skilled employees.

- **Employment Pass** – Reserved for highly skilled professionals in managerial, executive, or specialist roles with higher salary requirements.

To qualify for permanent residency, foreign nationals must demonstrate strong academic performance and professional achievements during their stay in Singapore. Graduates from Singaporean higher education institutions who secure employment may also be eligible.

Employers must ensure that applicants meet the Ministry of Manpower's (MOM) requirements, including minimum salary thresholds, before applying for a work pass. The specific type of work pass granted depends on factors such as salary, qualifications, and work experience.

Students on Tuition Grant Scheme

Students who have received admission under the 'Tuition Grant Scheme' are obligated to work for a Singapore-based company for at least three years after completing their studies. On the other hand, students who are not enrolled under the Tuition Grant Scheme can choose to work for any organization, anywhere, during or after completing their degree.

Job opportunities after graduation

Singaporean universities often integrate "Industrial Attachment" or internships (mandatory or optional, typically 5-6 months and often paid) into their programs, providing valuable practical experience. Stipend amounts vary by program.

Teaching Jobs: Fluency in English is advantageous for teaching positions in Singapore, as it's the primary language of education A TEFL qualification is generally required for public schools, and specific eligibility criteria may vary by employer.

Doctors/Physicians/Nursing: Doctoral graduates in Singapore in fields like nursing, physician practices, physiotherapy, and physician specialties are among the highest earners, with average salaries ranging from 15,100 SGD to 43,500 SGD monthly.

Engineering/IT/Data Analytics: Engineering and data science professionals are in high demand among international students, with average monthly salaries ranging from 7,920 to 14,500 SGD.

Pilots: Piloting, a highly responsible profession requiring intensive training, offers average salaries between 6,030 SGD and 19,700 SGD monthly.

College Professors: A career as a college professor demands perseverance and a comprehensive approach, with average monthly salaries ranging from 7,240 SGD to 23,700 SGD.

Orthodontists: Orthodontics is a lucrative field due to the demand for quality dental services, with average monthly salaries ranging from 8,150 SGD to 26,600 SGD.

Chapter 9

Studying in Dubai, UAE

Dubai, UAE, while famous for its architecture, also possesses a strong education system emphasizing research and innovation, with high-quality and accessible education as a priority.

The city offers diverse degree programs through internationally recognized universities and colleges, catering to various budgets and needs from pre-schools to universities. Its schools provide a wide array of curricula, including the UK National Curriculum, IB, CBSE, GCSE, IGSCE, Montessori, Cambridge, French, Australian, UAE MoE, Chinese, and Iranian systems.

A quality education in Dubai often leads to excellent job prospects, supported by its thriving economy (5th largest in the Middle East) with opportunities in finance, tourism, healthcare, and a growing presence of foreign companies. Notably, the technology and artificial intelligence sectors are projected to have significant growth potential.

As Dubai expands, it anticipates offering exceptional career opportunities in fields like Artificial Intelligence, Data Sciences, HR, Business Studies, Financial Analysis, and Engineering, making it an ideal destination for those seeking high-paying, future-proof employment.

Top universities in Dubai:

1. **Al Ghurair University (AGU):** A private university in Dubai International Academic City (DIAC), licensed by MOHESR. AGU offers bachelor's degrees through the University of Dubai (UD), Zayed University, and Biotechnology University College Dubai (BUC).

2. **The University of Dubai:** A globally and nationally accredited university in central Dubai established to address workforce skills gaps. It offers undergraduate degrees in business administration, management, marketing, finance,

banking, accounting, HR, entrepreneurship, economics, supply chain and logistics management, and IT.

3. **Zayed University:** A government-sponsored university with campuses in Abu Dhabi and two in Dubai. Its six colleges offer globally recognized undergraduate and postgraduate degrees in arts, business, communication and media sciences, education, sustainable sciences and humanities, and technological innovation.

4. **Biotechnology University College Dubai (BUC):** A MOHESR-accredited institution providing undergraduate and postgraduate programs in biotechnology, medical and pharmaceutical studies, environmental and agricultural studies, and petroleum and industrial studies.

5. **The Higher Colleges of Technology (HCT):** One of the UAE's largest higher education institutions, with over 55,000 graduates. HCT operates 17 campuses, including Dubai Men's College (DMC) and Dubai Women's College (DWC), both offering undergraduate business programs.

6. **The American University in Dubai (AUD):** A private university near Dubai Media City, Dubai Internet City, and the Palm Islands. Accredited by SACSCOC (U.S.) and UAE MOHESR, AUD offers diverse undergraduate and postgraduate programs in finance and accounting, business and management, engineering and information studies, and arts and humanities (postgraduate only).

7. **The University of Wollongong in Dubai (UOWD):** A private university in Dubai Knowledge Village, established as a branch of the University of Wollongong (Australia) in 1993. UOWD offers undergraduate and postgraduate programs in finance and accounting, business and management, engineering and information studies, and arts and humanities (postgraduate only).

8. **The British University in Dubai (BUiD):** A research-based postgraduate university in Dubai International Academic City, collaborating with leading UK universities. BUiD offers

MOHESR-accredited programs in business administration (MBA), informatics, and IT management.

9. **The American University in the Emirates (AUE):** A private university in Dubai International Academic City, licensed by the CAA. AUE collaborates with US and international universities, offering undergraduate and graduate programs (excluding PhD).

Dubai features a robust educational infrastructure with internationally accredited institutions providing undergraduate and postgraduate programs across various fields. These universities are equipped with modern facilities and experienced faculty, preparing graduates for successful careers.

Requirements for admission:

- Completed application form

- Proof of paying the application fee (if applicable)

- High school diploma (to apply for a Bachelor's)

- Bachelor's diploma (to apply for a Master's)

- Transcript of records

- Passport-sized photo(s)

- Copy of valid passport and/or personal ID

- Motivation letter.

How to Find the Right Program:

Students should carefully evaluate how their chosen program will impact their future careers. Researching a university's reputation, teaching methods, and employability opportunities is crucial. Key factors include global rankings, accreditation, international partnerships, and a research-driven curriculum.

While some students have a clear major in mind, others should thoroughly explore their options to ensure a fulfilling university experience by selecting an institution that aligns with their educational and professional goals.

Given the shift back to in-person learning, it's important to ensure the university has the technological infrastructure to support blended learning and offers flexibility in program delivery (blended, face-to-face, or fully online).

Scholarships in Dubai:

Several UAE organizations offer scholarships in specialized fields to support students' academic pursuits and contribute to the country's economic development.

The Masaar Scholarship: Offered by the Ministry of Finance and the Federal Authority for Government Human Resources, this scholarship provides financial aid for finance and accounting degrees, aiming to prepare graduates for employment at the Ministry of Finance. Eligibility requires a high school certificate (or equivalent) with a minimum 75% average or 3.0 GPA, graduation within the last three years, non-employment, and not receiving other simultaneous scholarships.

The Emirates Nuclear Energy Corporation (ENEC) Scholarship: ENEC offers scholarships for talented Emirati students pursuing Bachelor's or Master's degrees in Nuclear Engineering in partnership with Abu Dhabi Polytechnic. This program includes professional experience and interaction with specialists. Applicants must be UAE nationals under 22, Advanced Track high school graduates with at least 80%, and have an IELTS score of 5.5 or equivalent.

Abu Dhabi National Oil Company (ADNOC) Scholarship Program: ADNOC provides scholarships in fields like engineering, AI, finance management, and economics, both locally and internationally, to encourage study in support of the country's economic and industrial goals. Eligibility includes passing an interview with the ADNOC Scholarship Department, medical fitness, and a military service release letter (if applicable).

The ICT Fund's BETHA program: This program supports Emirati students in computer engineering, electronic engineering, computer science, and information technology for study in countries like the USA, UK, Australia, Japan, and the UAE. The ICT Fund aims to advance the ICT sector globally.

The Full Tuition Scholarship: This scholarship is awarded to undergraduate students demonstrating and maintaining excellent academic performance at UAEU, covering 100% of their tuition fees.

Partial Tuition Scholarships: UAE University offers incentive scholarships of up to 50% of tuition fees to exceptional high school graduates across various colleges (excluding Law, Literary track in Education, Arabic Programs in Humanities and Social Sciences, and Business and Economics). Eligibility requires a minimum of 90% in Grade 12 or equivalent, IELTS 6.5 (or equivalent), and a minimum score of 630 in Math SAT Subject Test (level 2) or 1400 in Math EmSAT (or equivalent).

These scholarships provide significant opportunities for students to pursue specialized academic goals and contribute to the UAE's development. Applicants should carefully review the specific eligibility criteria for each scholarship.

Student Eligibility Criteria for Applications:

To be eligible for admission and financial aid at UAEU, students generally need a minimum of 97% in their high school certificate (or equivalent), an IELTS score of at least 7 or an EmSAT English score of 1675, and a minimum Math SAT Subject Test (level 2) score of 680 or a Math EmSAT score of 1500 (unless applying to specific colleges). Different minimum scores apply for admission to the College of Law, the Literary track in the College of Education, Arabic Programs in the College of Humanities and Social Sciences, and the College of Business and Economics. Applicants to the College of Law, the Literary track in the College of Education, and Arabic Programs in the College of Humanities and Social Sciences must also achieve a minimum EmSAT Arabic score of 1350 or its equivalent.

Documents required for admission:

- Student's Birth Certificate

- Parent's Passports

- Parents' Residency Visas*

- Parent's Emirates IDs*

- Student's Emirates ID

- Student's Photo (Passport Size)

- Parents' Photo (Passport Size)

- Copy of a valid UAE Residence Visa.

- Previous Schengen, USA, or UK visa copy;

- Declaration of Value (or Statement of Comparability released by CIMEA);

- A pre-enrolment letter released by the university portal, or enrolment letter, if in pre-enrolment, is not required;

- A copy of the final academic qualification has been duly attested and apostilled.

- Proof of sufficient means of subsistence. A minimum of € 45

Permanent residency and extended visa options:

Student visa

International students can reside in the UAE for their studies either under the sponsorship of their parent, a UAE resident, or the university they are studying at. The university's student affairs department can assist in obtaining a student visa, which is valid for one year and renewable upon submission of proof of continuing studies. Family members of international students can also stay in the UAE as long as they can provide suitable housing. This initiative by the government aims to promote moral stability for the students. To be eligible for a UAE residence visa, individuals must fall under one of the categories outlined by the government:

- You will work in the UAE, under a governmental office, or in a private company.

- You will study in a UAE educational institution.

- You are the dependent of a UAE citizen or foreign resident (child, parent, maid, or a close relative)

- You have made an investment in the UAE

- You have purchased the property in the UAE

- You will retire in the UAE

Types of UAE Residence Visas:

UAE residence visas are categorized by the purpose of the visit. These include Work Visas (for employment), Student Visas (for foreign students enrolled in UAE institutions), Family Visas (for close relatives of citizens or residents), Investment Visas (long-term for substantial investment), and Retirement Visas (for eligible elderly foreigners). Additionally, the "Work Remotely from Dubai" program offers visas to foreign freelancers.

Job Opportunities in Dubai:

UAE students have various employment opportunities based on their skills and interests, including Graphic design, Social Media expert roles, Content writing and development, Medical assistant positions, Translators, Tour guides, Restaurant servers and waiters, Laundry and cleaning services, Home tutoring, Substitute teacher roles, Online jobs, and Sales management and monitoring.

Apart from scholarships, part-time job options are available.

Translation Work: Bilingual students can find freelance translation work through platforms like MotaWord and Gengo, as well as universities and banks. English and Arabic are most in demand in Dubai, with potential earnings of around 4,000 AED per month.

Benefits include flexible hours, competitive pay, and valuable resume-building experience.

Call Center Jobs: Working as a call center representative is another common part-time option, offering good pay and work experience, though it may involve routine tasks. Ideal candidates are international students proficient in English and those with customer service or call center experience. Students can earn between 2,000 to 3,500 AED per month. Companies like Oasis Group, AFIA Insurance, and Parker Connect frequently hire for these roles.

Chapter 10
Studying in Denmark

Denmark offers high-quality education, with five universities ranking among the top globally. Degrees are internationally recognized and prepare students well for their careers.

Contrary to common perception, studying in Denmark can be affordable, with some tuition fees starting at €6,000 per year. Merit-based scholarships are often available to attract accomplished students.

The Erasmus Mundus Scholarship Program, funded by the EU, is a significant opportunity for both EU and non-EU Master's and doctoral students, covering all expenses (tuition, travel, insurance) and providing a monthly living allowance. Applicants with strong academic and English proficiency are encouraged.

Denmark's higher education system is known for its innovative approach and high academic standards across various fields. Universities frequently collaborate with businesses and research institutes, providing students with industry insights. Many programs include credit-earning internships for practical experience.

Collaboration and inspiration are central to Danish education. Students often work in groups, even during exams and thesis projects. The system blends lectures and tutorials with innovative teaching methods focused on problem-solving. Problem-based learning and open debate encourage student participation and experimentation. The learning environment is welcoming and relaxed, with open discussions between students and teachers.

Denmark offers a welcoming and open-minded environment for international students, with a diverse student population fostering valuable networks and cultural exchange. It's considered a safe and tolerant country with rare instances of racism. While Danish is the primary language, 70% of the population speaks English, facilitating communication.

Leisure and entertainment options are abundant, including libraries, restaurants, and outdoor activities. Denmark is known as one of the happiest nations, partly due to the positive attitude of its people. Regular social and community events encourage connection and enjoyment outside of studies.

Healthcare facilities in Denmark are widely available and affordable, providing peace of mind for international students. These factors make Denmark an attractive destination for high-quality education in a welcoming and enjoyable setting.

Top 10 Universities in Denmark

1. **University of Copenhagen:** Ranked 76th globally and Denmark's top university (founded in 1479), it emphasizes research-based teaching and has an excellent faculty-student ratio. Committed to sustainability, it has 39,000 students and is known as a green campus.

2. **Technical University of Denmark (DTU):** Climbing to 103rd in world rankings, DTU excels in natural and technical sciences, particularly Environmental Science (45th globally in 2020). It's known for attracting top faculty, reflected in its strong student-faculty ratio (25th) and international faculty ranking (62nd).

3. **Aarhus University:** Ranked 147th (down two places in 2020), Aarhus University has a significant international student population (12% from over 120 nationalities). It's renowned for its research, especially in Archaeology (27th globally in 2020), and focuses on research-based learning with a welcoming environment for international students.

4. **Aalborg University:** Rising to joint 305th in 2020 (up 19 places), Aalborg University scores highly for its international faculty, with 15% international students. It offers a real-world learning approach backed by strong research, with campuses in Aalborg, Esbjerg, and Copenhagen.

5. **University of Southern Denmark:** Ranked joint 353rd (up four places in 2020), this university has a high proportion of

international students (one in five). It focuses on developing transferable skills applicable across various industries and has campuses in multiple Danish cities.

6. **Copenhagen Business School (CBS):** CBS provides an excellent academic and research environment alongside extracurricular activities, leadership opportunities, and career support. It's a strong training ground for business careers, with experienced professionals and a curriculum blending rigorous assessments and practical training.

7. **Roskilde University:** Established to disseminate knowledge innovatively, Roskilde University is known for academic excellence and inclusive education. It emphasizes transparency and democracy in knowledge-sharing, contributing to society through innovative and experimental research.

8. **IT University of Copenhagen:** This university focuses on delivering cutting-edge education in digital design, computer science, and IT. It aims to generate profound knowledge in the industry, fostering groundbreaking technology and collaborating with public sectors and international researchers to encourage student entrepreneurship.

9. **Royal Danish Academy - Education with a Social Mission:** This academy (Architecture, Design, and Conservation) aims to develop students who can drive positive societal change through their skills. It employs a productive teaching strategy and fosters an inclusive academic community for the collaborative creation of a more equitable world.

10. **University College Lillebaelt - Large Institution with Global Reach:** With over 11,000 students across its campuses, it's the seventh-largest educational institution in Denmark. Offering diverse courses and programs, it welcomes exchange students globally and aims to be a hub for growth and welfare, developing solutions with significant societal impact.

To be admitted to a Danish college, your prior education must meet Danish high school standards. However, relevant vocational qualifications may suffice for specific programs like Academy Profession degrees. Beyond general requirements, you must also meet specific program requirements, including subject level, grades, and overall average marks, which should be checked on the institution's website. If you don't meet the criteria, supplementary courses (only in Danish and won't improve your GPA) might be an option. Language proficiency in Danish or English may also be required before program commencement.

Application Process:

Once you meet the qualifications, you can begin the application process early to allow time for document gathering. Undergraduate applications are centrally coordinated but evaluated locally. You don't apply directly to a single institution. You can apply for up to eight programs simultaneously but will receive only one offer for your highest-priority program. For each program, you must print and sign a signature page generated on www.optagelse.dk containing an application ID needed by the institution. If applying to multiple programs at the same institution, send multiple signed signature pages. Diplomas and other documents must be uploaded to www.optagelse.dk by the specified deadlines and requirements. You can modify your applications (priority, deletion) until July 5th at 12 PM on the website.

Picking The Right Program:

Choosing a program can be challenging. Consider your interests, but also the impact of hands-on learning opportunities like labs, field trips, internships, and study abroad programs offered by universities. Research these experiential options to align with your learning style. Also, carefully examine the type of degree awarded, as programs with the same name can vary. Narrow your search by focusing on universities offering courses matching your interests and goals, and review the required courses for valuable insights into the curriculum. When considering finances, budget carefully, as university costs can be significant. Investigate paid co-op or internship programs offered by universities to help with expenses. Remember that your skills and potential are generally more valued by employers than just the degree name. Ultimately, select a program based on your interests, preferred learning style, degree type, required courses, and available financing options.

Scholarships for Studying in Denmark:

1. **Nordplus Program:** Offers scholarships to international students for undergraduate, postgraduate, and doctoral studies at Nordic partner institutions in Denmark.

2. **Erasmus Program:** A popular scholarship for Bachelor's, Master's, and doctoral students across Europe, including Denmark. The application is through a Danish university.

3. **Erasmus Mundus/Joint Master Degree Program:** Provides full funding for international Master's students in Denmark enrolled in select Erasmus Mundus Joint Master degree courses.

4. **Government Scholarships for UG, PG, and PhD Studies:** A significant scholarship supported by the Danish Ministry of Higher Education and Science, available to international students at undergraduate, postgraduate, and doctoral levels through Denmark's eight universities.

Other International Scholarships (Mentioned for Context):

5. **Berklee on the Road Clinics Scholarship:** Berklee College of Music offers aid to a significant portion of incoming students and provides this scholarship based on performance in their global clinics.

6. **6G Excellence Scholarships:** A collaboration between EURECOM and the OpenAirInterface Software Alliance for motivated students pursuing a Master of Science in Intelligent Communication Systems.

7. **Drs. Anthony and Joanne Edmonds Study Abroad Scholarship:** Provides financial aid to a Ball State History student studying abroad in odd years, alternating with the Honors College.

8. **Spreadsheet Gladiator Scholarship:** Coefficient offers an annual scholarship to a college student pursuing a degree in Business, Computer Science, or Communications.

9. **Pinsky Law New Venture Development Scholarship:** Supports aspiring entrepreneurs pursuing new ventures.

Visa Process

To apply for a Danish study permit, you must first be accepted into an accredited Danish institution and pay the application fee. Next, gather all necessary documents, including a formal admission letter, academic program details, your passport and photos, a completed ST1 form, proof of language proficiency, evidence of sufficient financial resources, details of your living arrangements, the application fee payment receipt, and proof of travel insurance.

Within 14 days of submitting your application, you'll need to have your biometric data recorded at a Danish diplomatic mission, application center, or police station. The standard processing time for a Danish student visa is approximately two months, but it can be longer for certain nationalities, including students from Nigeria, Pakistan, Kenya, and Ghana. Therefore, it's crucial to plan ahead and allow ample time for the application process.

PR

To qualify for permanent residency in Denmark, you must be over 18 years old, still meet the criteria for your current residence permit, and be a resident in Denmark when your PR application is decided. If you are outside Denmark, you must return.

You need at least eight years of uninterrupted legal residency in Denmark at the time of the decision. Conviction of crimes with a sentence exceeding six months disqualifies you. You must have no overdue payments for the Social Service Act or active Social Policy Act benefits, child support paid in advance, daycare payments, overpaid housing benefits, housing subsidy loans, taxes, and levies.

You must not have received certain social benefits within four years before applying or until PR is granted. Accepting a declaration of residence and self-support (included in the application) is mandatory.

Employment is required; you should have a non-terminated, permanent position or be self-employed at the time of the decision, with proof of continued employment or self-employment. You must not have obstructed the establishment of your identity by providing false information or using falsified documents.

Passing the Danish language test 2 or an equivalent higher-level Danish exam is necessary. You also need to have been employed for at least three years and six months in regular employment (minimum 30 hours/week or 120 hours/month paid employment, equivalent self-employment, work in a spouse's business, sick leave, holiday, family care leave, parental leave within employment terms). Flexjob may also qualify under specific conditions.

Job Opportunities

Denmark has a strong and diverse economy with a low unemployment rate of 2.7%. The country's location makes it an important distribution point for Europe, and its top exports include pharmaceuticals, medical equipment, iron and steel, food products, textiles, clothing, and electronics.

Chapter 11

Studying in the Netherlands

The Netherlands has a long-standing and highly regarded higher education system, with many universities consistently ranking among the world's best. This makes it a popular study abroad destination, particularly for students from developing countries, drawn by its welcoming and inclusive environment, affordable tuition fees, and numerous English-language programs.

Dutch society is characterized by its "live and let live" philosophy, fostering a diverse and accepting atmosphere. This core value of inclusiveness further enhances the Netherlands' appeal to international students.

Graduates from Dutch universities often desire to stay in the country due to its strong economy, financial growth, and ample job opportunities. The Netherlands is a flourishing tech and startup hub, with the government actively promoting innovation and the recruitment of skilled foreign workers, leading to a diverse and dynamic workforce.

Top Universities in the Netherlands.

1. Wageningen University & Research (WUR)

Specializing in agricultural and environmental sciences, Wageningen University & Research offers a variety of undergraduate and postgraduate programs in Dutch and English. With over 27% of its student body coming from overseas, it is a popular choice for international students.

2. University of Amsterdam (UoA)

Founded in 1632, the University of Amsterdam is the country's third oldest and largest institution in the Netherlands. It is highly regarded worldwide for its arts, humanities, and social sciences programs.

3. Utrecht University

Established in 1636, Utrecht University is a prominent research university with students and staff of 118 different nationalities. It is one of the largest universities in the Netherlands and offers a wide range of academic programs.

4. Delft University of Technology (DUT)

Delft University of Technology is the country's largest and oldest public technical university. It was established as a royal academy for civil engineers, and it is known for its engineering and technology programs.

5. University of Groningen

Inaugurated in 1614, the University of Groningen offers a diverse range of English-taught bachelor's and master's degrees across 11 faculties and nine graduate schools. It is located in the city of Groningen.

6. Leiden University

Founded in 1575 as a Protestant university, Leiden University is a public research institution in Leiden. It is one of the oldest universities in the Netherlands and is regarded highly for its research and academic programs.

7. Erasmus University College

Erasmus University College is a public liberal arts college located in Rotterdam. It is the undergraduate honors college of the Erasmus University Rotterdam, offering a BSc degree in Liberal Arts & Sciences.

8. Radboud University Nijmegen

Located in Nijmegen, Radboud University is a public research university named after Saint Radboud, a 9th-century Dutch bishop known for his intellect and support of the underprivileged.

9. Vrije Universiteit Amsterdam

Founded in 1880, Vrije Universiteit Amsterdam is a public research university offering a range of academic programs. It is one of the two largest publicly funded research universities in Amsterdam.

10. Maastricht University

Established in 1976, Maastricht University is the second youngest of the 13 Dutch universities. It has a diverse student population, with over 56% of its students coming from abroad.

Entry Requirements:

Admission to Dutch higher education programs is typically determined by the institution and requires specific qualifications. You can compare your diplomas to the minimum requirements on the Nuffic website, which also assists institutions in evaluating foreign qualifications. English proficiency is essential, requiring a passing score on tests like IELTS (minimum 6) or TOEFL (minimum 550 paper-based or 213 internet-based); some institutions may accept other tests like Cambridge English. If your qualifications don't initially meet the requirements, extra preparation might allow admission the following year; contact the university's international office to verify degree recognition. Non-EU/EEA or Swiss citizens may need a residence permit, and programs taught in Dutch require a good command of the language. Foreign diplomas often need a minimum average of 7-7.5. Admission requirements vary by university and subject, and some programs have selection procedures due to limited seats.

Finding the Right Program:

When choosing between a university of applied sciences and a research university, consider your career goals. For applied professions like engineering, IT, logistics, or travel management, universities of applied sciences offer practical training and potential internships leading to jobs. For scientific research or teaching, research universities known for producing Nobel laureates and significant discoveries might be more suitable. Consult international university rankings to assess their reputation, but remember that a high overall ranking doesn't always mean leadership in your specific field of interest (e.g., Tilburg University's strong business and economics programs despite a lower overall rank). Communicate with university representatives to understand their content delivery methods and determine if your desired industry prioritizes theoretical knowledge or practical experience. Identify key program factors like duration, credit for existing experience, desired skills, and the importance of work experience to make an informed decision.

Scholarships and Funding

1. Orange Knowledge Program

The Orange Knowledge Program is designed to enhance the capacity, knowledge, and quality of individuals and organizations in higher and vocational education and other fields related to priority themes in participating countries.

2. University of Twente Scholarships (UTS)

The University of Twente Scholarships are available for outstanding students from EU/EEA and non-EU/EEA countries who apply for a graduate program (MSc) at the University of Twente.

3. Leiden University Excellence Scholarships (LexS)

Leiden University Excellence Scholarships are awarded to exceptional non-EEA and non-EFTA students who are enrolled in a full-time master's degree program at Leiden University.

4. Holland Scholarship for Non-EEA International Students

The Holland Scholarship is funded by the Dutch Ministry of Education, Culture, and Science. It is intended for international students from outside the European Economic Area (EEA) who wish to pursue a bachelor's or master's degree at one of the Dutch research universities or universities of applied sciences in Holland.

5. Utrecht Excellence Scholarships for International Students

The Utrecht Excellence Scholarship provides an opportunity, especially for international students from outside the EEA, to pursue a master's degree in selected fields at Utrecht University.

6. VU Amsterdam Fellowship Program for International Students

The VU Fellowship Program offers talented prospective non-EU/EEA students a unique chance to pursue a master's degree at Vrije Universiteit Amsterdam.

7. Maastricht University Holland High Potential Scholarships for International Students

Maastricht University offers the Holland-High Potential Scholarship to highly talented students from outside the European Union (EU) who have been admitted to a master's program at UM. The scholarship includes a tuition fee waiver, a monthly stipend, and a Holland Scholarship.

PR Requirements:

To qualify for permanent residency in the Netherlands, several general requirements must be met:

- A valid Dutch residence permit held for at least five consecutive years (with some exceptions).

- Children must be at least 13 years old and have held a valid residence permit since age 8; only years from age eight count towards the five-year period.

- The main residence must have been in the Netherlands for the entire five-year period.

- All residence permit extensions must have been timely, and all permit requirements must have been met and continue to be met.

- A valid, non-temporary residence permit must currently be held.

- The applicant must not pose a threat to public order or national security.

- No incorrect or incomplete information should have been provided during the current residence permit application, which would have led to rejection if it had been accurate.

- The income criterion must be fulfilled.

- Registration in the Personal Records Database (BRP) at the local town hall is necessary.

- The civic integration examination must have been passed (or exemption criteria met).

- Applicants born in the Netherlands who are now 18 or under and have always lived there since starting before age three can only be rejected if they pose a threat to public order or national security.

When applying for permanent residency, the IND will first check the requirements for a long-term EU resident permit without requiring action from the applicant. Holding a long-term EU resident permit can simplify applying for residency in other EU countries, though their specific requirements still apply.

Job Opportunities:

The Netherlands is an appealing destination for expats seeking career growth and a high quality of life. While salaries might be lower than in some countries, opportunities for building a successful career exist, particularly in major cities like Amsterdam and Rotterdam, which offer diverse international job prospects.

The Dutch job market currently has a high demand for professionals in engineering, health and public services, financial services, IT, project management, research, hospitality, construction, education, and science and research. These sectors have numerous open positions, making it easier for expats to find employment in their fields. With a high standard of living, excellent work-life balance, and a welcoming environment for international workers, the Netherlands is an attractive option for career advancement and experiencing a new culture.

Chapter 12

Studying in Sweden

Sweden attracts students for higher education due to its natural beauty and other appealing factors. The average tuition for a Master's program is around USD 14,500 per year, with Bachelor's programs generally being less expensive. The monthly cost of living for students is approximately USD 900, varying by location. Part-time work opportunities are available with consultancy assistance.

Upon completing their studies, students can apply to extend their residence permit for at least six months to seek employment in Sweden. Many degree programs include internships, offering valuable practical experience and networking possibilities.

Sweden is home to numerous multinational corporations like IKEA, TetraPak, Volvo, Ericsson, AstraZeneca, Securitas, Spotify, and H&M, making internships or full-time positions with these companies highly sought after by students.

Top Ten Universities in Sweden

1. Karolinska Institute

Located in Solna, Stockholm County, the Karolinska Institute, also known as the Royal Caroline Institute, is a renowned medical university focusing on research and education. It has approximately 6,000 students and is located close to the Karolinska University Hospital.

2. Lund University

Established in 1666, Lund University (LU) is a public research university that consistently ranks among the world's top institutions. It is situated in Lund in the province of Scania—a city in southern Sweden near Denmark and Germany. With over 41,000 officially registered students across multiple campuses, LU is one of the Nordic region's largest educational and research institutions.

3. Uppsala University

Founded in 1477, Uppsala University is the oldest university in Sweden and Scandinavia. It is highly regarded for its research and comprises nine faculties distributed over three domains: Humanities and Social Sciences, Medicine and Pharmacy, and Science and Technology. The university hosts more than 52,000 students and roughly 2,200 doctoral students, along with a significant international student population of 12%.

4. KTH Royal Institute of Technology

As Sweden's largest and oldest technical university, KTH Royal Institute of Technology is a leading institution in natural sciences, engineering, architecture, industrial management, and urban planning. It plays a significant role in technical research and education in the country.

5. Stockholm University

Founded in 1878, Stockholm University is one of Scandinavia's oldest and largest universities. It offers diverse subjects and continues the tradition of providing public mathematics, physics, chemistry, and geology lectures.

6. Linkoping University

Ranked at #330 among the Best Global Universities, Linkoping University is known for its exceptional education and research across various disciplines.

7. Chalmers University of Technology

The Chalmers University of Technology holds the #337 spot among the Best Global Universities. It is known for its high performance in various areas, as determined by widely accepted indicators of excellence.

8. Swedish University of Agricultural Sciences

Ranked at #356 among the Best Global Universities, the Swedish University of Agricultural Sciences excels in agricultural sciences based on widely accepted indicators of excellence.

9. Umea University

On the list of Best Global Universities, Umea University ranked 366. It is a well-recognized institution because of how well it performs on several excellence indices.

10. University of Gothenburg

The University of Gothenburg is a public institution whose history goes back to 1891. The Gothenburg University was established in 1954 in Gothenburg, one of Sweden's largest cities, and it offers various facilities throughout the city.

Entry Requirements:

For undergraduate programs in Sweden, applicants need a high school diploma with a minimum of 60% marks and must be at least 18 years old. English proficiency equivalent to Swedish upper secondary English Course 6 is required. Additionally, completion of mathematics courses comparable to about 10 years of Swedish university-level mathematics is necessary.

For Master's programs, a Bachelor's degree from an internationally recognized university or equivalent to the Swedish *Kandidatexamen* is required. Good English proficiency, typically demonstrated through IELTS or TOEFL scores, is also necessary.

Finding the Right Program:

Conduct comprehensive online research to identify courses and universities in Sweden that align with your interests. Explore the diverse approaches and institutions available. Visit the official university websites for detailed program and course information. Consider your preferred university, desired program, and suitable location. Ensure you are well informed about the specific admission requirements for your chosen course and university.

Scholarships and Funding:

Swedish Institute Scholarships for Global Professionals: The Swedish Institute (SI) offers fully funded scholarships for Master's studies at Swedish higher education institutions. In 2025, approximately 200 scholarships are available. These scholarships cover full tuition fees and provide a monthly living allowance of SEK 12,000, health insurance, and round-trip airfare of SEK 15,000.

Visby Program: This scholarship is for Master's students from specific nations. It provides a full tuition fee waiver, a living allowance of SEK 9,000 per month, health insurance, and SEK 5,000 for flights.

Lund University Global Scholarship Program: A merit-based program offering partial or full tuition fee waivers to exceptional non-EU/EEA students at Lund University.

The Jönköping University Scholarship: Rewards outstanding students with exceptional academic performance in Bachelor's or Master's programs with a 30% tuition fee reduction.

Halmstad University Scholarships: Provides international students from outside the EU/EEA/Switzerland with scholarships amounting to a 25% or 50% tuition fee waiver.

BTH Scholarship: Blekinge Institute of Technology offers international students a 50% tuition fee reduction scholarship.

Chalmers University Avancez Scholarships: A merit-based scholarship for non-EU international students at Chalmers University of Technology, offering a 75% tuition fee reduction for two-year programs, with potential additional reductions for top students.

Dalarna University Scholarship: Offers tuition fee reductions ranging from 10% to 50%, depending on the specific scholarship awarded.

GIH Scholarship: The Swedish School of Sport and Health Sciences (GIH) provides full tuition fee waivers for undergraduate and postgraduate courses in sports and health.

Karlstad University Global Scholarship: For academically exceptional students from outside Switzerland, the EU, and the EEA, offering tuition fee reductions of 25%, 50%, 75%, or 100%.

Here's the condensed information about documentation for Swedish university applications and PR/Citizenship:

Documentation for University Application:

The **application form** (online or offline) must be completed carefully. **English language test scores** (TOEFL, IELTS, PTE) are required for Master's and business programs to demonstrate proficiency. **Academic certificates** (SSC, intermediate, Bachelor's, Master's degrees, transcripts, project work details) are necessary to prove educational qualifications. The **Statement of Purpose (SOP)** is a crucial essay outlining career goals, research objectives, reasons for course and university choice, post-course plans, and personal interests. A **Letter of Recommendation** from someone who can assess your qualities and capabilities is typically required. For **business programs, relevant work experience documents (joining letters, salary slips, employment certificates) are often needed, though they are not usually needed** for undergraduate applicants. A well-prepared **resume** detailing educational background and skills is essential. Correctly sized and up-to-date **photographs** must be included. Any **additional documents** showcasing paper presentations, organizational skills, or other achievements can strengthen your application. The university will verify your documents and profile before issuing an offer letter. If requirements aren't met or authenticity is doubted, the application can be rejected. Upon receiving an offer, you can apply for a student visa with the necessary documents.

PR / Citizenship:

The most efficient way to apply for a Swedish study residence permit is online through the Swedish Migration Agency. Obtaining a permit before entering Sweden is crucial.

For **Permanent Residence (PR)**, if you hold a research residence permit, you need at least four years within the last seven. Time with a work or doctoral studies permit may also count. General requirements include meeting continued residence permit conditions, residing in Sweden with a valid permit for a specific duration, demonstrating financial self-sufficiency, and maintaining a law-abiding lifestyle. The first two requirements vary based on your current permit type, while the last two are universal. These PR requirements should be considered alongside the requirements for extending a residence permit. Different rules apply for those with residence permits for upper secondary level studies or job search after such studies.

Job Opportunities

Sweden is renowned for offering some of the most exceptional benefits in the world, encompassing healthcare, education, and generous vacation allowances. As a result, the country boasts promising job opportunities, making it an appealing destination for individuals seeking high living standards and social welfare. Despite Sweden's high tax rates, the prospect of pursuing a lucrative career abroad in this nation remains enticing. With competitive salaries, excellent perks, and a growing array of possibilities, Sweden has garnered a formidable reputation for its workforce. The country has diligently built robust and efficient institutions that offer employees long-term prospects, reflecting the collective efforts of its people.

Chapter 13

Studying in Switzerland

Switzerland, a welcoming European nation, is an attractive destination for international students due to its exceptional universities, groundbreaking research, and investment in cutting-edge industries. Students in Zurich and Geneva enjoy access to a rich cultural scene, including art galleries, museums, theaters, and live music. Its proximity to the Alps also allows for easy exploration of stunning mountain landscapes.

Switzerland's major cities are global hubs for finance, technology, and innovation, boasting a cosmopolitan atmosphere due to their diverse international populations. The country has four official languages: German, French, Italian, and Romansh, with regional variations. English is also widely spoken, especially in business, universities, and cities like Zurich, Geneva, and Bern.

While most university degrees are taught in French and German, many Swiss universities offer programs in English, attracting a significant number of international students and creating vibrant, multicultural campuses. For instance, the University of Geneva has around 16,000 students, with approximately 40% being international.

Top 10 Universities in Switzerland:

1. **ETH Zurich - Swiss Federal Institute of Technology:** Fosters independent thinking and encourages outstanding research, connecting globally and pioneering solutions to global challenges.

2. **Swiss Federal Institute of Technology in Lausanne (EPFL):** Epitomizes Swiss innovation in research and education, achieving remarkable results and fostering a vibrant entrepreneurial ecosystem with international collaborations

3. **University of Applied Sciences and Arts Western Switzerland (HES-SO):** Plays a key role in the socio-

103

economic and cultural development of Western Switzerland, comprising six faculties and a network of higher education schools recognized nationally and internationally.

4. **University of Basel:** Switzerland's oldest university (founded 1460), renowned internationally for its outstanding achievements in research and teaching with a rich history of over 550 years.

5. **University of Bern:** Highly regarded for its top-quality education and excellence in teaching and research across diverse disciplines, offering a connected academic setting within the city.

6. **University of Fribourg:** A dynamic hub for learning, research, employment, and events, significantly influencing the region's commercial and cultural life through its innovative spirit.

7. **University of Geneva (UNIGE):** Founded in 1559, committed to critical thinking, teaching, dialogue, and research, with a diverse student body from over 150 countries, offering a wide range of programs.

8. **University of Lausanne (UNIL):** Offers an international atmosphere with a significant proportion of international students and teaching staff.

9. **University of Neuchâtel (UniNE):** Emphasizes high pedagogical standards for professors to share knowledge effectively and inspiringly.

10. **University of St. Gallen (HSG):** Evolved from a "business academy" into a distinguished university with over a century of history, providing a blend of research and practical experience with a strong culture of excellence.

Entry Requirements:

Applying to Swiss universities is straightforward, but remember these key points: explore diverse, research-focused study options;

carefully review programs and degree levels to align with your goals; thoroughly understand entry requirements (specific criteria for medicine, dentistry, and veterinary degrees); and seek available scholarships for international students.

How to Apply: Complete the online application on the university's website, pay the application fees within the deadline, and upload all required supporting documents (academic transcripts, language proficiency certificates, CVs, motivation letters, ID copies, passport photos).

Language Requirements: Switzerland's official teaching languages are German, French, and Italian, with many universities offering programs in English, German, and French. Accepted language proficiency tests include DSH, TestDaF, ÖSD, TELC (German), DELF, DALF (French), and IELTS or TOEFL (English). Some universities offer their own language tests.

Swiss Universities Admission Requirements: Prepare required documents: application form copy, passport photos, ID copies, academic transcripts, high school/Bachelor's diploma, language certificate, CV, fee payment proof, and a personal essay. Apply directly through each university's admission portal on their website, as there's no centralized system. Doctoral program applicants may need a supervisor's letter and translated certificates/transcripts (into French, English, German, or Italian), along with an explanation of the previous university's grading system.

Finding the Right Program:

Allow ample time for careful consideration when selecting your study path, institution, and location.

Phase 1: Researching and Deciding: Identify your needs and preferences, evaluate institution and course profiles aligning with your interests, and compile a list of 10-15 institutions for detailed information. Review this information and request further details before finalizing your choice.

Phase 2: Applying: Meticulously complete the application process, ensuring no important aspects are missed. Consult institutions for required documents and prepare for potential interviews. Apply to accredited institutions, verifying their standards on their official websites.

Admission Requirements at Different Levels of Study For Bachelor's Studies: The primary requirement is a Swiss secondary high-school leaving certificate (Matura) or an equivalent foreign certificate. Students without a recognized certificate may need to take a university entrance exam.

Scholarships:

- **Swiss Excellence Scholarships:** The Swiss Government offers scholarships annually for young researchers (Master's or PhD completed) and foreign artists (Bachelor's degree) to foster international exchange and research collaboration.

- **ETH Zurich Excellence Scholarships:** ETH Zurich provides scholarships, mentorship, and networking for Master's students, covering the entire program and living costs. The ETH-D Scholarship includes a partial stipend and potential additional funding.

- **University of Zurich Scholarships:** The largest Swiss university offers a wide range of academic options and provides scholarships for international students.

- **University of Bern International Scholarships:** Recognizes excellent teaching and research, offering scholarships to international students.

- **Ecole Polytechnique Fédérale de Lausanne (EPFL) Scholarships:** EPFL offers numerous scholarship opportunities for Bachelor's, Master's, and doctoral students.

- **University of Basel International Scholarships:** Offers scholarships through its Senate Scholarship Committee in addition to cantonal contributions for international students.

- **University of Lausanne Scholarships:** Provides merit-based scholarships, Swiss Government Scholarships, and World Bank Scholarships for international students.

- **University of Geneva Scholarships:** Switzerland's second-largest university prioritizes teaching, research, and community service and offers scholarships to its diverse international student body.

- **University of Lausanne Master's Grants for Foreign Students:** Offers monthly grants (CHF 1600) to international Master's students for a duration not exceeding the program's minimum prescribed period.

- **Geneva Academy of International Humanitarian Law and Human Rights Scholarships:** Provides partial and full scholarships covering tuition and/or living expenses for its LLM and Master of Advanced Studies programs.

PR / Citizenship:

For **Swiss Citizenship** through naturalization, you need a minimum of 10 years of residency in Switzerland, a valid residence permit, proficiency in a Swiss official language, and strong integration into Swiss society.

For **Permanent Residence (PR)**, the primary requirement is the duration of stay with a valid residence permit ("B" or "L" permit), typically 10 years. However, EU/EFTA citizens, American and Canadian citizens, and spouses/children (12-18) of Swiss citizens or "C" permit holders may be eligible after five years. Specific requirements for a "C" permit vary by canton; contact the local cantonal immigration office for accurate steps. The application generally involves a form that provides a valid ID, proof of address, evidence of the existing residence permit, and verification of meeting requirements like language certificates. Switzerland issues biometric permanent residence permits (credit card design) with a microchip for biometric data and Schengen area visa-free travel.

Job Opportunities

Switzerland has become a sought-after destination for expatriates in search of employment opportunities. While finding a job can be challenging, Switzerland offers some of Europe's highest minimum wages and average salaries. However, it is essential to note that the Swiss work culture expects high dedication and effort.

Chapter 14

Studying in the Russian Federation

According to the OECD, Russia boasts a highly educated population, exceeding that of Canada, Japan, Israel, and the USA, with over half holding higher education qualifications. The country also attracts over 200,000 international students from 168 countries.

Russian higher education is known for its excellence, particularly in engineering and science, with graduates being well-regarded by employers globally. The system offers a wide variety of options, with nearly 450 state-accredited universities and about 17,500 degree programs across all academic levels. Increasingly, courses are available in English for international students.

Russian universities embrace cultural diversity, with around twelve percent of students being international, providing opportunities for global networking and cultural exposure.

Top 10 Universities:

1. **Lomonosov Moscow State University (MSU):** A prominent public research university in Moscow encompassing numerous research institutes, faculties, departments, and branches.

2. **Novosibirsk State University:** A well-established public research university in Novosibirsk focused on integrating education and science with early student involvement in research and leading scientists as teachers.

3. **Tomsk State University (TSU):** A distinguished public research university in Tomsk, the first university in Asian Russia and the pioneering Russian university east of the Volga.

4. **Moscow Institute of Physics and Technology (MIPT):** A renowned public research university in Moscow Oblast

specializing in theoretical and applied physics, applied mathematics, and related fields.

5. **St Petersburg University:** A prestigious public research university in Saint Petersburg, founded in 1724, with a focus on fundamental research in science, engineering, and humanities.

6. **Peoples' Friendship University of Russia (RUDN University):** A distinguished public research university in Moscow named after Patrice Lumumba.

7. **Higher School of Economics (HSE University):** A reputable public research university founded in 1992 and headquartered in Moscow.

8. **National Research Nuclear University MEPhI (Moscow Engineering Physics Institute):** A technical university in Russia, originally established in 1942.

9. **Sechenov First Moscow State Medical University (MSMU):** The oldest medical university in Russia, located in Moscow, with notable international rankings.

10. **Peter the Great St. Petersburg Polytechnic University (SPbPU):** A distinguished technical university in Saint Petersburg with a history of name changes.

Entry Requirements:

Russia has relatively lenient admission requirements for international students with an education equivalent to general secondary education. All documents must be translated into Russian. An official invitation from Russia is needed to obtain a visa from the Russian Embassy. Upon arrival, a mandatory (compensated) medical examination confirms no health obstacles to studying. The initial exam costs around USD 58. Health services are available on a compensatory basis, and compulsory medical insurance (around 85 EUR annually) is required for emergency medical assistance. Annual medical examinations (approximately USD 35) are also mandatory.

Finding the Right Program:

Research programs and universities several months in advance. Identify your interests and thoroughly research relevant courses and subjects on university websites. Note admission requirements, available courses, and deadlines. Shortlist potential institutions aligned with your interests and check their admission criteria. Consider visiting campuses to learn more about courses and institutions and speak with faculty and students. After research and visits, make a well-informed final decision, considering affordability, location, finances, program engagement, and alignment with your academic and career goals. Submit your application on time, checking specific requirements and necessary documents with the chosen university.

Scholarships:

- **Berklee on the Road Clinics:** Educational sessions by Berklee College of Music for aspiring music professionals.

- **Drs. Anthony and Joanne Edmonds Study Abroad Scholarship:** Biennial financial aid for a Department of History student studying abroad.

- **Spreadsheet Gladiator Scholarship:** Annual USD 1,500 scholarship for college students in Business, Computer Science, or Communications who extensively use spreadsheets.

- **Pinsky Law New Venture Development Scholarship:** Supports students interested in entrepreneurship, recognizing the financial challenges of new ventures.

- **Anonymous Hope Fund:** Supports personal proposals, with a high percentage of legitimate submissions receiving funding.

- **Fighting Bullying With Technology:** Supports students affected by bullying, those actively fighting it, or those using technology to create safer and more inclusive school/community environments.

- **Erasmus Mundus Joint Masters Scholarships:** EU-supported scholarships for jointly recognized Master's degrees, promoting excellence and internationalization.

- **Education Future International Scholarship:** A scholarship fund supported by past winners to aid future students.

- **F.L. McEwen Scholarship:** Prioritizes students with research interests in sustainable agriculture and related extracurricular involvement.

- **Ethel Rose Charney Scholarship in the Human/Animal Bond:** Supports research related to the human-animal bond, available for Master's and doctoral students (renewable annually).

Documents Required Upon Arrival:

Upon acceptance and arrival in Russia, international students must prepare:

- **Educational Certificate:** Including a comprehensive list of studied subjects and marks.

- **Medical Certificate:** Obtained from an official public health service in your home country.

- **AIDS Test Certificate:** Issued by an official public health service in your home country.

- **Copy of Birth Notification.**

- **10 passport-sized photos (4 x 6 cm).**

- **National Passport with Russian Study Visa.**

- **Notarized Translations:** All documents must be translated into Russian and notarized.

The application vetting process concludes upon submission of all required documents. Successful students are typically notified within 2-3 weeks and receive a formal acceptance letter after the tuition down payment. Registration and course enrollment follow.

Citizenship / PR:

To become a **Russian citizen**, you must be born on Russian soil to Russian citizens or permanent resident parents or live continuously in Russia with a temporary residency permit for at least five years.

Foreign nationals can apply for Russian nationality after residing in Russia for at least five years with a **permanent residence permit**. Obtaining a permanent residence permit is the initial step towards citizenship and offers benefits similar to those of Russian citizens.

The Russian permanent residence permit is valid for five years and renewable, issued by the Russian General Directorate of Migratory Affairs.

Russian citizenship can be obtained through naturalization or by birth if parents have Russian origins. While a permanent residence permit is an option, Russian citizenship offers advantages like the ability to establish a business or work as a sole trader, full access to social services, and visa-free travel to and from Russia.

Job Opportunities:

Awareness of earning potential in Russia is beneficial for those seeking high-paying sectors. Some of the highest-paying jobs include:

- Ship Captain — 500,000 RUB

- Aircraft Commander — 320,000 RUB

- Chief Technologist (gold mining) — 312,000 RUB

- Head Coach (ice hockey) — 300,000 RUB

- Construction Site Manager — 250,000 RUB

- Dentist — 200,000 RUB

- Risk Manager — 200,000 RUB

- Electrical Engineer — 195,000 RUB

- IT Analyst — 190,000 RUB

- Aircraft Co-pilot — 180,000 RUB

Securing a well-paying job in Russia, especially for foreigners, can be challenging, but it is possible. Explore online recruitment platforms, such as LinkedIn, or direct CV and cover letter submissions to companies. Persistence and proactivity in the job search can increase your chances of a high-paying offer.

Chapter 15

Studying in Germany

Studying in Europe is a coveted aspiration for many students, and Germany stands out as one of the most popular destinations, especially for Indian students seeking education abroad. Renowned for its prestigious universities, Germany offers a dream destination for students with its world-class education, multicultural environment, affordable lifestyle, picturesque landscapes, vibrant nightlife, and delectable cuisine.

In Germany, international universities provide diverse courses, including opportunities for research and skill-based training, allowing students to explore new educational avenues and broaden their horizons. Some programs even allow students to pursue multiple courses simultaneously, enabling them to follow their passions while studying at the university.

An overseas college experience in Germany fosters interactions with individuals not just from Germany but from around the globe, leading to the development of valuable intercultural communication skills. One essential aspect of studying in Germany is learning German since English may not be commonly spoken, particularly outside academic circles. Proficiency in German can significantly enhance job prospects, particularly in fields like international relations and diplomacy, where foreign language expertise is highly valued.

Studying abroad offers students a competitive edge when entering the professional world. It demonstrates to employers qualities like courage, adaptability, cultural awareness, and understanding of different work environments and perspectives. These attributes make international degree holders highly sought after by employers, leading to unmatched job opportunities and attractive pay packages, especially from top tech companies.

Top 10 Universities

1. Technical University of Munich (TUM)

TUM derives its strength from the excellence in research and education of its seven TUM Schools and fosters transdisciplinary innovations through mission-driven Integrative Research Institutes. Embracing rapid societal changes in the digitalization era, TUM has revolutionized the concept of engineering by integrating natural and life sciences, medicine, business management, humanities, and social sciences.

2. LMU Munich (Ludwig Maximilian University of Munich)

As one of Europe's foremost research universities with a history spanning 500 years, LMU prides itself on its excellence in teaching and research across diverse fields. From humanities and cultural studies to law, economics, social sciences, medicine, and natural sciences, LMU's academic pursuits are comprehensive and impactful.

3. Heidelberg University

Heidelberg University offers 36 undergraduate courses, four graduate programs, and 16 minors, offering students various academic options. The university's innovative honors program, "The Life of the Mind," enables students to study thematic areas. With a strong international presence and a long-standing exchange program, Heidelberg fosters global connections and embraces a diverse international student body.

4. Charité - Universitätsmedizin Berlin

With a remarkable legacy of producing more than half of Germany's Nobel prize winners in medicine and physiology, Charité is a prestigious medical university. Its history spans 300 years, and today, it is a significant employer in Berlin, boasting a turnover of €1.5 billion per annum and housing 3,700 doctors.

5. Humboldt University of Berlin (HU Berlin)

Recognized as a pioneering higher education institution in Europe, HU Berlin owes its reputation to Wilhelm von Humboldt's model, emphasizing a close relationship between research and teaching—a model widely adopted by universities worldwide.

6. University of Tübingen (Eberhard Karls University of Tübingen)

As a respected academic authority in humanities, natural sciences, and theology, the University of Tübingen is significant among traditional German university towns. Renowned for its boat trips and the stunning architecture of its old town, Hölderlin.

7. University of Bonn

Ranked among the world's leading research universities, the University of Bonn is home to a diverse community of over 35,000 students and 4,500 academic staff. With strategic partnerships with 70 universities worldwide, the university fosters a strong international atmosphere, welcoming around 4,000 international students annually.

8. Free University of Berlin

Hosting a vibrant student body of over 32,000 and offering over 150 degree programs, the Free University of Berlin is a hub of academic excellence. With collaborative research centers, an extensive academic staff, and international partnerships, the university maintains a global outlook through its liaison offices in major cities worldwide.

9. RWTH Aachen University

Renowned for its strong ties with industry, RWTH Aachen has developed a European equivalent of Silicon Valley around its campus, attracting substantial external funding for its researchers. The university has also nurtured a thriving ecosystem of university spinoff companies and engineering firms.

10. University of Freiburg

With 180 undergraduate, graduate, and professional degree programs spread across 11 faculties, the University of Freiburg strongly emphasizes interdisciplinary and innovative studies. Students can enrich their bachelor's degree with a multidisciplinary year, fostering a well-rounded and forward-thinking educational experience.

Entry Requirements

Germany offers a limited selection of undergraduate courses solely taught in English. However, some programs provide instruction in German and English, offering an excellent opportunity for Bachelor's students to improve their German language skills while pursuing their studies. On the other hand, graduate students will find a growing array of English-taught degree options in Germany.

For admission to German universities, two main German language tests are universally accepted: the DSH (German language exam for university entrance), which is available only in Germany, and the TestDaF, which can be taken in 90 countries worldwide.

If you plan to enroll in a course partly taught in English, you must submit an English language certificate. The most popular English language proficiency tests accepted by German universities include PTE Academic, IELTS Academic, TOEFL iBT, and Duolingo.

Picking the Right Program

Discovering the right subject for your university program requires thoughtful consideration. Start by reflecting on your interests and passions. Identify the subjects that excited you the most during your high school years, as they can offer valuable insights into potential areas of study. Additionally, evaluate the field's worth in terms of the time and resources you'll invest, considering its relevance to your long-term goals and aspirations. Research the job prospects after completing the course to ensure they align with your career objectives.

Once you have narrowed down a subject, delve into the course content to ensure it covers topics that genuinely engage you and suit your learning style. If you're uncertain about a specific course, don't hesitate to contact the university for a copy of the syllabus or seek further information.

Beyond selecting a subject, you'll also need to determine the type of degree you want to pursue in higher education. Universities and colleges offer three main types of degrees: undergraduate

(Bachelor's), graduate (Master's), and doctoral (PhD). Bachelor's degrees generally take three or four years, while master's degrees require one or two years of study. Doctoral programs can take up to five years, and they are ideal for those interested in research-oriented careers. Shorter courses like certificates and diplomas lasting less than a year are also available for specialized skill development. Choose the degree that best aligns with your career objectives and academic ambitions.

Scholarships

Friedrich Ebert Stiftung Scholarship:

The Friedrich Ebert Stiftung is a non-profit political foundation in Berlin, Germany, focusing on promoting social democracy both within the country and globally. The scholarship financially supports students who value social democracy and are pursuing undergraduate programs, graduate studies, or PhDs. It includes a monthly stipend of €774, study fee coverage of €300, health insurance contribution, and other benefits.

Heinrich Boll Scholarships for International Students:

The Heinrich Boll Foundation, an independent political foundation established in 1997, is committed to promoting political education in Germany and internationally. Their scholarship supports graduate students and PhD candidates with monthly stipends of €850 and €1200, respectively, enabling them to pursue their studies.

Konrad-Adenauer-Stiftung Scholarship:

The Konrad-Adenauer-Stiftung is a political foundation that fosters democracy, dialogue, and cooperation between Germany and other countries. The scholarship program supports students worldwide pursuing master's and doctoral degrees in Germany. It provides financial assistance, including monthly stipends of €861 for master's students and €1,200 for Ph.D. students, along with healthcare insurance, family allowance, and children's allowance.

Erasmus Scholarship Programs in Germany:

The Erasmus scholarship program offers full tuition and travel coverage to international postgraduate students pursuing master's degrees in Germany. This opportunity allows students to benefit from an international education experience.

Bayer Foundation Scholarship:

The Bayer Foundation offers scholarships to both domestic and international students pursuing master's and doctoral degrees in Germany. The scholarship, which can provide funding of up to $10,000, supports research in various critical areas of study.

Marie Curie International Incoming Fellowships (IIF) For Developing Countries:

This scholarship is open to international students pursuing a PhD in their respective fields. It offers funding of up to $15,000 per year to support students' research and education.

Mawista Scholarship:

Unlike traditional scholarships, the Mawista Scholarship focuses on supporting students who often receive less attention. It provides a one-time payment of $3,000 to students pursuing bachelor's, master's, and doctoral degrees.

Rosa Luxemburg Stiftung Scholarships for International Students:

The Rosa-Luxemburg-Stiftung Scholarship Department awards scholarships at all levels of education, including bachelor's, master's, and PhD's. Recipients are chosen based on their exceptional academic achievements, making it a prestigious opportunity for highly qualified students.

Deutschlandstipendium Program (DAAD Scholarship):

Funded by the federal government and private sponsors, the Deutschlandstipendium Program, or DAAD Scholarship, provides financial support to undergraduate and graduate students pursuing their studies in Germany. It includes a monthly allowance of €300.

DAAD Helmut-Schmidt Masters Scholarships for Public Policy and Good Governance:

The DAAD Helmut Schmidt Masters Scholarships for Public Policy and Good Governance Program is a government-funded scholarship opportunity for international students pursuing master's degrees in Germany. It offers full tuition fee coverage, a monthly allowance of 931 €, and additional benefits such as health insurance and travel fees.

Required Documents

Each university sets its admission criteria, but generally, most of the following will be included:

- Certified copy of a high-school diploma or a previously completed degree

- Translation of the course modules and grades

- Passport photo(s)

- Copy of your passport

- Proof of language proficiency – German and/or English

- Motivation letter

- Application fee

Citizenship / PR

Gaining German citizenship is not universally possible; it is contingent upon meeting specific conditions under three general instances. These occurrences are naturalization, right of blood (Jus Sanguinis), and right of soil (Jus Soli).

Citizenship by naturalization is attainable when an individual fulfills specific requirements set by the German government, making them eligible to apply for German citizenship. On the other hand, citizenship by right of blood or Jus Sanguinis applies to individuals who are direct descendants of German citizens, limited to their parents and excluding other relatives. Citizenship by right of soil or Jus Soli is acquired when an individual is born within the borders of Germany, on German soil.

For all individuals, except for EU, EEA, or Swiss nationals, fulfilling the prescribed requirements and fitting into one of these categories is essential to obtaining German citizenship. While these instances may seem straightforward, each has its distinct rules and regulations that must be carefully followed. It is important to note that gathering the necessary documentation and fulfilling all requirements within the designated timeframe can present significant challenges.

Job Opportunities

Germany boasts one of the most international economies globally, ranking alongside the USA, China, and Japan. As the top trading nation in the European Union, it is renowned for embracing innovation and facilitating international exports within its borders. The country's robust economy, exceptional infrastructure, and high income levels make it a sought-after destination for foreigners, including international students.

Germany's allure also extends to expats, as many companies offer attractive employee benefits and perks that surpass those found in many other European nations. The country's job market provides excellent employment opportunities for individuals from all over the world.

Chapter 16

Studying in Italy

Italy's rich cultural heritage, spanning art, architecture, cuisine, romanticism, and music, has significantly impacted global culture. Studying abroad in Italy offers a unique chance to broaden your global perspective and deepen your appreciation for diverse cultures.

Italian culture includes the tradition of *riposo*, an afternoon break where locals nap after lunch during the hottest part of the day. This practice allows students to experience and integrate into the local lifestyle.

Study abroad programs in Italy are highly popular due to its captivating cuisine, scenic landscapes, historical sites, and world-renowned museums. With a wide array of programs available, students can explore fields like fashion, creative writing, and visual art. The best programs cater to specific majors, including communications, design, languages, medicine, and architecture. For example, a program in Florence might focus on humanities and social sciences, while one in Rome could offer enriching experiences in film and media studies.

Italy also has a high-quality education system, home to the prestigious University of Bologna—the world's oldest university and a long-standing center of excellence in art, science, and higher education. The University of Padova is similarly renowned for its science and engineering programs.

Furthermore, even for those not majoring in languages, learning Italian offers significant advantages. It improves communication while traveling and provides a competitive edge in fields such as foreign relations, tourism, and marketing.

Top Ten Universities

1. **University of Bologna (Università di Bologna)**

The University of Bologna, founded in 1088, is one of the world's oldest and most prestigious universities. It offers a wide range of programs and strongly emphasizes research and innovation. With its historic campus and esteemed faculty, the university attracts students from all over the globe.

2. University of Milan (Università degli Studi di Milano)

The University of Milan is renowned for its excellence in research and teaching across various disciplines. It was founded in 1924 and has since grown into one of Italy's leading universities, fostering a vibrant academic community and providing a diverse and challenging learning environment.

3. Sapienza University of Rome (Sapienza Università di Roma)

Sapienza is the largest university in Europe and one of the oldest in the world, dating back to 1303. Located in the heart of Rome, it boasts a rich academic tradition and offers a vast array of programs, attracting students from different cultural backgrounds.

4. Politecnico di Milano

Politecnico di Milano is a prominent technical university focusing on engineering, architecture, and design. It excels in research and industry collaborations, providing students with cutting-edge facilities and opportunities for practical experience.

5. University of Padua (Università degli Studi di Padova)

The University of Padua, founded in 1222, is another of Europe's oldest universities. It is known for its comprehensive research programs and outstanding contributions to various fields of study, including medicine, law, and the sciences.

6. University of Florence (Università degli Studi di Firenze)

The University of Florence is a leading institution in Italy, offering a wide range of arts, humanities, social sciences, and natural sciences programs. Its historic campus and vibrant cultural scene attract students seeking a dynamic learning experience.

7. University of Pisa (Università di Pisa)

The University of Pisa is renowned for its contributions to science and technology. It was founded in 1343 and has a strong reputation for research excellence in physics, engineering, and mathematics.

8. University of Turin (Università degli Studi di Torino)

The University of Turin is one of the oldest universities in Italy, dating back to 1404. It offers a wide array of programs and is notably recognized for its law, economics, and humanities research.

9. University of Naples Federico II (Università degli Studi di Napoli Federico II)

As one of the oldest public universities in the world (founded in 1224), the University of Naples Federico II boasts a rich history and a diverse range of academic programs, attracting students from various cultural backgrounds.

10. University of Trento (Università degli Studi di Trento)

The University of Trento is known for its high-quality teaching and research, especially in economics, social sciences, and information technology. It offers a welcoming and modern learning environment for students from Italy and abroad.

Entry Requirements

The entry requirements for Italian universities can vary depending on the level of study (undergraduate, postgraduate, or doctoral), the specific university and program, and whether the applicant is an EU/EEA/Swiss citizen or an international student. Below are the general entry requirements for each level of study:

Undergraduate (Bachelor's) Programs:

Academic Qualifications: Students must have completed their secondary education (high school or equivalent) and obtained a valid diploma that allows access to higher education in their home country.

Language Proficiency: For programs taught in Italian, students must demonstrate proficiency in the Italian language by providing an internationally recognized language certificate (e.g., CILS, CELI) or by passing a language test organized by the university. Some universities may offer undergraduate programs in English, and in such cases, students may need to provide proof of English proficiency (e.g., IELTS, TOEFL).

University Admission Test (if applicable): Some degree programs may require students to take an entrance exam or an assessment test to evaluate their aptitude and suitability for the course.

Postgraduate (Master's) Programs:

Academic Qualifications: Students must hold a relevant bachelor's degree or an equivalent qualification from a recognized institution. The degree should be related to the field of study they intend to pursue at the master's level.

Language Proficiency: Similar to undergraduate programs, language proficiency in Italian or English (depending on the language of instruction) is required.

Letters of Recommendation and Statement of Purpose: Many postgraduate programs require students to submit letters of recommendation from professors or employers and a statement of purpose explaining their academic and career goals.

Entrance Exam or Interview (if applicable): Some master's programs may have additional entry requirements, such as an entrance exam or an interview, to assess the candidate's knowledge and skills.

Finding the Right Program

Start by identifying your interests, strengths, and career aspirations. Consider what subjects you enjoy studying and what career path you envision for yourself. Understanding your passions and long-term goals will guide your program selection.

You can research the rankings and reputation of Italian universities and their specific programs. Look for universities known for excellence in your chosen field of study. Consider factors like faculty expertise, research opportunities, and industry partnerships.

It will help if you determine whether you are comfortable studying Italian or prefer an English-centric program. Many universities offer courses in English, especially at the postgraduate level, to cater to international students.

Review the curriculum of the programs you are interested in. Check if the courses offered align with your academic interests and if any specializations or concentrations match your career goals.

You have to ensure that the university and your chosen program are accredited and recognized nationally and internationally. Accredited programs generally meet specific quality standards.

Consider the location of the university and its proximity to amenities, cultural attractions, and potential job opportunities. Additionally, examine the available campus facilities, libraries, laboratories, and extracurricular activities.

Top Ten Scholarships

Italian Government Scholarships for Foreign Students

The Italian Ministry of Foreign Affairs offers scholarships to international students from various countries. These scholarships cover different academic levels, including undergraduate, postgraduate, and doctoral programs. They aim to promote cultural exchange and collaboration between Italy and other countries.

EDISU Piemonte Scholarships

EDISU Piemonte provides scholarships to domestic and international students studying at public universities in the Piedmont region of Italy. Scholarships are awarded based on financial need, academic merit, and other specific criteria.

Politecnico di Milano Scholarships

Politecnico di Milano, one of Italy's top technical universities, offers scholarships to international students pursuing undergraduate, master's, and doctoral programs. These scholarships may cover tuition fees, living expenses, or both.

Bocconi University Scholarships for International Students

Bocconi University in Milan offers various scholarships to outstanding international students applying to undergraduate, master's, and doctoral programs. These scholarships recognize academic excellence and may provide full or partial tuition waivers.

Università Cattolica del Sacro Cuore Scholarships

Università Cattolica del Sacro Cuore provides scholarships for international students who wish to study at the university's campuses in Milan, Piacenza, Cremona, and Rome. The scholarships are available for bachelor's and master's degree programs.

Scuola Normale Superiore PhD Scholarships

Scuola Normale Superiore (SNS) is a prestigious institution offering fully-funded PhD scholarships in various disciplines. These scholarships cover tuition fees, accommodation, and a stipend for living expenses.

University of Bologna Study Grants for International Students

The University of Bologna offers study grants and tuition fee waivers to deserving international students enrolled in bachelor's or master's programs.

Padua International Excellence Scholarship Program

The University of Padua offers scholarships to highly talented international students applying for degree programs. These scholarships support outstanding academic achievements and research potential.

NABA Scholarships for International Students

NABA (Nuova Accademia di Belle Arti) in Milan provides scholarships and financial aid to international students enrolling in design, fashion, and arts programs. These scholarships are merit-based.

Istituto Europeo di Design (IED) Scholarships

IED offers scholarships to international students pursuing various design courses at their campuses across Italy. Scholarships are awarded based on academic excellence and creative potential.

Required Documents

Application Form: Complete and submit the university's official application form for the desired program of study.

Academic Transcripts: You must provide official transcripts or academic records from your previous educational institutions, including high school for undergraduate applicants and bachelor's degree for postgraduate applicants.

Diploma or Degree Certificate: A copy of your high school diploma or bachelor's degree certificate, depending on the level of study you are applying for.

Language Proficiency Test Results: Proof of language proficiency in either Italian or English, depending on the language of instruction of your chosen program. This may include language test scores such as TOEFL or IELTS for English and CILS or CELI for Italian.

Passport or Identity Document: You must submit a copy of a valid passport or identification document to verify your identity and nationality.

Passport-sized Photographs: Provide recent passport-sized photographs per the university's specifications.

Specific requirements may vary from one university to another or even between different programs within the same university.

Citizenship / PR

The process of obtaining Italian citizenship can be complex and varies depending on individual circumstances. There are several pathways to acquiring Italian citizenship, including descent (*jure sanguinis*), marriage to an Italian citizen, naturalization, and special provisions for certain groups, such as stateless individuals or refugees.

Citizenship by Descent (Jure Sanguinis):

If you have Italian ancestors, you may be eligible for citizenship by descent. The process involves proving your lineage through birth certificates, marriage certificates, and other relevant documents, usually dating back to the Italian ancestor. Requirements and eligibility criteria may differ depending on the generation and the date of emigration of your Italian ancestor.

Citizenship by Marriage:

If you are married to an Italian citizen, you may be eligible for citizenship after a certain period of marriage, usually two years if you reside in Italy or three years if you live abroad. You must meet specific requirements and demonstrate sufficient knowledge of the Italian language.

Citizenship by Naturalization:

Foreign nationals legally residing in Italy for a certain period (usually ten years, but it may vary based on circumstances) may be eligible for citizenship by naturalization. During this period, you must have a valid residence permit and demonstrate integration into Italian society, knowledge of the Italian language, and sufficient financial stability.

It's important to note that Italian citizenship laws are subject to change, and the requirements can be complex, depending on your situation. Therefore, it is highly recommended to seek professional advice from an immigration lawyer or consult the official website of the Italian Ministry of Foreign Affairs for the most up-to-date and accurate information regarding the citizenship process.

Job Opportunities

Italy offers a diverse range of job opportunities across various industries. Some of the key sectors with employment opportunities in Italy include:

Tourism and Hospitality

Italy is a top tourist destination with a rich cultural heritage and picturesque landscapes. Job opportunities are available in hotels, restaurants, tour agencies, and other tourism-related businesses.

Manufacturing

Italy has a strong manufacturing industry known for luxury fashion, automotive, machinery, and design. Jobs are available in production, engineering, design, and management roles.

Finance and Banking

As a major financial hub, Milan offers job opportunities in the banking, finance, investment, and insurance sectors.

Chapter 17

Studying in Spain

Each year, thousands of international students choose Spain for its 76 universities, drawn by the promise of an enriching experience. Studying in Spain encourages the development of new perspectives on life and the world.

Spain boasts a rich and diverse culture with a long history, vibrant traditions, and a lively arts scene. Studying there offers the opportunity to immerse yourself in this culture, learn the language, and gain a deeper understanding of Spanish history and its way of life.

As one of the world's most spoken languages, studying in Spain provides an immersive environment to significantly improve your Spanish skills, which can be invaluable both personally and professionally. Spain is home to several renowned universities and educational institutions, offering access to high-quality academic programs and courses with a unique European viewpoint.

Furthermore, Spain offers diverse study programs across various disciplines, including art, history, science, engineering, business, and more, allowing you to find a program that aligns with your academic and career aspirations.

Studying abroad also exposes you to a global network of students and professionals, building international connections that can be beneficial for future career opportunities and collaborations.

The Top Universities in Spain

1. **University of Barcelona (Universitat de Barcelona):** One of Spain's oldest, it's known for extensive research and diverse academic programs in the vibrant city of Barcelona.
2. **Complutense University of Madrid (Universidad Complutense de Madrid):** Located in Madrid, this large and prestigious university offers a wide array of programs with a strong emphasis on research and academic innovation.
3. **Autonomous University of Barcelona (Universitat Autònoma de Barcelona):** Known for its beautiful campus

and strong research focus, it offers diverse academic programs near Barcelona and is well-regarded in various fields.

4. **Pompeu Fabra University (Universitat Pompeu Fabra):** A relatively young university recognized for high-quality teaching and research, particularly strong in social sciences, humanities, and communication studies.

5. **University of Navarra (Universidad de Navarra):** This private university in Pamplona is known for rigorous academic programs and research, especially in business, law, and communication.

6. **University of Granada (Universidad de Granada):** With a rich history, this university is known for academic excellence and cultural significance, offering a wide range of disciplines in Granada.

7. **Carlos III University of Madrid (Universidad Carlos III de Madrid):** This modern university emphasizes social sciences and humanities, offering innovative programs in law, economics, and political science with a dynamic international student body.

8. **University of Valencia (Universitat de València):** Established in the 16th century, it's one of Spain's oldest, recognized for contributions to science, arts, and humanities, with a blend of historical and modern architecture.

9. **IE University:** A private institution with campuses in Madrid and Segovia, known for its business, law, and social sciences programs and a dynamic international learning environment.

10. **Polytechnic University of Catalonia (Universitat Politècnica de Catalunya):** Specializing in engineering, architecture, and technology, this university is a leader in technical education and research with multiple campuses.

Entry Requirements

Entry requirements for Spanish universities vary by study level and the specific institution/program.

Undergraduate Programs:

- **Educational Qualification:** Typically requires a high school diploma or equivalent.

- **Language Proficiency:** If the program is in Spanish, you'll likely need to demonstrate proficiency through standardized tests like DELE.

- **Entrance Exams:** Some competitive programs (e.g., medicine, engineering) may require entrance exams.

- **Application Process:** Apply via the university's admissions portal, providing educational history, a personal statement, and other required documents.

Postgraduate Programs (Master's and PhD):

- **Educational Qualification:** A recognized bachelor's degree or equivalent from an accredited institution is needed.

- **Language Proficiency:** Proof of Spanish proficiency (e.g., DELE) may be required for Spanish-taught programs.

- **Supporting Documents:** Official transcripts and letters of recommendation are usually necessary.

- **Statement of Purpose:** Many programs require a statement outlining your academic and professional goals.

- **Entrance Exams/Interviews:** Some programs may include specific entrance exams or interviews.

- **PhD Applicants:** You may need to submit a research proposal.

- **Application Process:** Apply through the university's admissions portal with all required documents and information.

Finding the Right Program

To find the perfect study program in a Spanish university, follow a systematic approach:

1. **Self-Assessment:** Reflect on your interests, career goals, and academic strengths.

2. **Research:** Explore Spanish university websites, focusing on program offerings, faculty, and facilities. Align programs with your interests and academic objectives, considering both specialized and interdisciplinary options. Prioritize accredited institutions with a strong reputation in your field. University rankings can offer some general insights.

3. **Language of Instruction:** Determine if the program is in English or Spanish and assess your language proficiency accordingly.

4. **Admission Requirements:** Carefully review the specific prerequisites for each program, including academic qualifications, entrance exams, recommendation letters, and other required documents.

5. **Location:** Consider the city and region of the university, taking into account climate, cost of living, cultural aspects, and potential career opportunities.

6. **Financial Considerations:** Estimate tuition costs, living expenses, and additional fees. Research available scholarships, grants, and financial aid for international students.

7. **Seek Guidance:** Consult with school counselors, educators, or education consultants for expert advice tailored to your academic background and goals.

Scholarships

1. **Erasmus+ Scholarship:** This European Union program offers scholarships for study abroad in European countries, including Spain, promoting international mobility and collaboration.
2. **La Caixa Foundation Scholarship:** Provides highly competitive postgraduate scholarships (Master's and PhD) in Spain, supporting academic excellence.
3. **Spanish Government Scholarships (Becas MAEC-AECID):** Offered by the Spanish Ministry of Foreign Affairs, European Union, and Cooperation for international students

pursuing postgraduate studies, research, and cultural exchanges in Spain.

4. **ICETEX Scholarship for Colombian Students:** Specifically for Colombian students wishing to study in Spain, funded by the Colombian Institute of Educational Credit and Technical Studies Abroad (ICETEX).

5. **DAAD Scholarship for Spanish Universities:** The German Academic Exchange Service (DAAD) offers scholarships for German students to study in Spain across various fields and academic levels.

6. **Agencia Española de Cooperación Internacional (AECID) Scholarships:** Provides scholarships for students from developing countries to pursue higher education and research in Spain, focusing on development-related disciplines.

7. **University-Specific Scholarships:** Many Spanish universities have their own scholarships for international students, potentially covering tuition, living expenses, or both. Check individual university websites for details.

8. **Santander Scholarships:** Santander Bank partners with various universities to offer scholarships to international students in Spain, often supporting mobility, research, or academic excellence.

9. **Fulbright Program in Spain:** Offers scholarships for U.S. citizens to study, teach, or research in Spain, fostering cultural exchange and academic collaboration.

10. **European Union Scholarships for Developing Countries:** The EU offers scholarships for students from developing countries through programs like Erasmus Mundus, supporting academic mobility and capacity building.

European Union Scholarships for Developing Countries

The European Union offers scholarships for students from developing countries through various programs like Erasmus Mundus. These scholarships support academic mobility and capacity building.

Required Documents

- Application Form

- Educational Documents:

- High School Diploma or Equivalent

- Bachelor's Degree Certificate

- Transcripts

- Language Proficiency

- Curriculum Vitae (CV) or Resume

- Statement of Purpose (SOP) or Personal Statement

- Letters of Recommendation

- Passport Copy

- Passport-Sized Photographs

- Application Fee

- Entrance Exam Scores

- Portfolio (if applicable)

- Proof of Financial Support

- Health Insurance

Citizenship / PR

The citizenship process in Spain involves several steps and requirements for individuals who wish to become Spanish citizens. It's important to note that the process can be complex and may change over time, so it's advisable to consult official government sources or legal professionals for the most up-to-date information.

Residency Requirements:

To apply for Spanish citizenship, you typically must have legally resided in Spain for a certain period. The residency requirement may

vary depending on your circumstances, such as whether you are from
a Spanish-speaking country or if you are a refugee.

Legal Residency Status:

You need to have legal residency status in Spain. This usually
means having a valid residence permit or similar authorization to live
in Spain.

Language Proficiency:

Depending on your circumstances, you may need to demonstrate
a certain level of proficiency in Spanish. This requirement can be
waived for citizens of Spanish-speaking countries.

Integration and Cultural Knowledge:

Applicants may need to demonstrate their integration into Spanish
society and show an understanding of Spanish culture, history, and
social values.

Renunciation of Previous Citizenship:

Spain generally requires applicants to renounce their previous
citizenship(s) as part of the process. However, some countries allow
dual citizenship, so it's important to understand the rules in your home
country.

Background Checks and Character Requirements:

Spanish authorities conduct background checks and assess the
applicant's character, criminal history, and overall behavior

Documentation:

You will need to provide various documents, such as birth
certificates, marriage certificates (if applicable), proof of residence,
language proficiency certificates, and other relevant paperwork.

Application Submission:

Once you have met the requirements, you can submit your
citizenship application to the relevant authorities. The application

process includes filling out forms and providing the required documentation.

Processing and Approval:

After submitting your application, it will be reviewed by the appropriate authorities. The processing time can vary, and you may be required to attend interviews or provide additional information.

Oath of Allegiance:

If your application is approved, you must take an oath of allegiance to Spain.

Citizenship Grant and Documentation:

Upon completing the process successfully, you will be granted Spanish citizenship. You will receive a naturalization certificate and can apply for a Spanish passport.

Key Job Sectors:

- **Tourism and Hospitality:** As a popular tourist destination, Spain offers numerous opportunities in hotels, restaurants, travel agencies, and related services.

- **Technology and IT:** The growing tech sector, especially in Barcelona and Madrid, provides positions in software development, data analysis, and IT services.

- **Engineering and Construction:** Ongoing infrastructure and urban development projects create demand for civil engineers, architects, and construction professionals.

- **Healthcare:** There's a need for doctors, nurses, and medical staff in both public and private healthcare.

- **Finance and Banking:** Major cities like Madrid have a strong financial sector with opportunities in banking, finance, and related services.

- **Manufacturing and Automotive:** Spain's automotive industry (e.g., Seat) and manufacturing sector offer roles in engineering, production, and logistics.

- **Agribusiness:** The agriculture sector provides opportunities in farming, food production, and related industries.

- **Language Services:** Proficiency in English is valuable for roles in translation, interpretation, content creation, and language training.

- **Creative Industries:** Spain's rich cultural scene in design, fashion, media, and arts offers opportunities for creative professionals.

- **Consulting and Business Services:** Management consulting, business analysis, and professional services sectors also provide employment options.

Job availability can differ by region, with larger cities like Madrid, Barcelona, Valencia, and Bilbao typically offering more opportunities due to their economic and cultural importance. Fluency in Spanish is often beneficial, particularly for roles involving communication with local clients and colleagues.

Chapter 18

Studying in France

Studying abroad in France offers a wealth of enriching experiences beyond academics. Immersing yourself in its renowned culture, history, art, and cuisine fosters a deeper global understanding. Engaging with local communities and mastering French enhances communication skills and cross-cultural competence.

France's esteemed educational institutions provide top-tier academic opportunities across diverse disciplines. Its central European location also allows for convenient travel to neighboring countries, exposing you to a continent rich in traditions and landscapes.

Navigating daily life amidst architectural wonders and picturesque scenery cultivates independence and resilience, honing personal and academic skills. This journey broadens your horizons, allowing you to carry the essence of France's charm and a lasting global perspective.

Top 10 Universities:

1. **Sorbonne University:** A prestigious institution with over 750 years of history, known for humanities, social sciences, and natural sciences.

2. **École Normale Supérieure (ENS Paris):** Renowned for its rigorous academic environment and production of eminent scholars across science, humanities, and social sciences.

3. **École Polytechnique:** A prestigious engineering school ("X") known for rigorous education and a strong focus on mathematics and sciences, producing top engineers and scientists.

4. **Pierre and Marie Curie University (UPMC):** A leading institution in science and medicine, offering a wide range of programs in various scientific disciplines.

5. **Paris Sciences et Lettres (PSL) University:** A collective of renowned institutions, including École Normale Supérieure and Collège de France, known for interdisciplinary programs fostering innovation and creativity.

6. **HEC Paris:** A prestigious business school recognized for its MBA and executive education programs and strong international reputation.

7. **University of Paris-Sud (Paris 11):** A leading research-oriented institution known for excellence in science and technology, with a strong focus on physics, chemistry, and engineering.

8. **Sciences Po Paris:** Specializing in social sciences and political studies, emphasizing critical thinking and international relations, preparing students for careers in politics, diplomacy, and academia.

9. **University of Strasbourg:** One of the oldest universities globally, offering diverse programs with a strong focus on research and innovation.

10. **L'Université Grenoble Alpes:** Recognized for its strengths in science, engineering, and technology, situated in the French Alps, offering a unique academic and outdoor environment.

Entry Requirements:

University entry requirements in France vary by study level, program, and university.

Undergraduate Programs:

- **High School Diploma or Equivalent:** Completion of high school or equivalent is necessary.

- **Language Proficiency:** For French-taught programs, demonstrating proficiency through DELF/DALF or TCF is usually required.

- **Application via Parcoursup:** Most undergraduate programs at public universities require application through the Parcoursup platform.

Postgraduate Programs:

- **Bachelor's Degree or Equivalent:** A bachelor's degree from a recognized institution is generally required for Master's programs.

- **Language Proficiency:** Proof of French proficiency (DELF/DALF or TCF) for French-taught programs or English proficiency (TOEFL or IELTS) for English-taught programs may be needed.

- **Academic Transcripts and References:** These are typically required to support your application.

- **Application Platforms:** Postgraduate applications may be submitted through university portals or platforms like Campus France.

It's crucial to research the specific program and university for detailed admission criteria, as requirements can vary significantly, and meeting minimum requirements doesn't guarantee admission due to program competitiveness.

Finding the Right Program

Finding the right study program in France requires careful research that is aligned with your educational and career goals.

Begin by defining your academic and professional objectives, including the degree level (Bachelor's, Master's, or PhD) and your specific field of interest. This will help narrow your search.

Next, explore French universities offering relevant programs, prioritizing those with strong academic reputations in your chosen field.

Consider your preferred language of instruction, as many universities offer programs in both French and English. Choose the option that best suits your language skills.

Utilize online resources like Campus France and university websites for detailed program information. Search engines such as Campus France, Eduniversal, and MastersPortal allow you to filter and compare programs based on your preferences.

While not the only factor, university rankings from respected sources like QS World University Rankings and Times Higher Education can provide insights into program quality.

Carefully review program descriptions to understand the course content and ensure it aligns with your academic interests. Also, admission requirements, including academic prerequisites and language proficiency, must be checked. Note any additional required materials, such as a statement of purpose or portfolio.

For further guidance, contact university advisors or French consulates in your country. They can provide clarification and guidance on the application process.

Based on your research, create a shortlist of programs that match your goals and preferences. Prepare the necessary documents and submit your applications before the deadlines.

Finally, remain open-minded, as excellent opportunities may arise in unexpected places.

Scholarships:

- **Eiffel Excellence Scholarship Program:** Offered by the French Ministry for Europe and Foreign Affairs for Master's and PhD degrees in fields like engineering, economics, and social sciences, covering tuition, living expenses, and travel.

- **French Government Scholarships (Eiffel Campus France Scholarships):** Provides scholarships for Master's and PhD international students, covering tuition, a monthly stipend, and other benefits, aiming to attract high-achieving individuals.

- **Erasmus+ Scholarships:** An EU program offering scholarships for international study and mobility, including exchange programs, internships, and joint Master's degrees at participating European universities in France.

- **Charpak Scholarship:** Offered by the Embassy of France in India for Indian students pursuing Master's and PhD programs, covering tuition, living expenses, and health insurance.

- **Ampère Excellence Scholarships:** Awarded by ENS de Lyon to outstanding international students for Master's or PhD programs, covering tuition and providing a monthly stipend.

- **A*midex Scholarship:** Available to international students at Aix-Marseille University pursuing Master's or PhD degrees in the university's research areas, covering tuition and providing a stipend.

- **INSEAD Scholarships:** A renowned business school offering various scholarships based on merit, diversity, and need for its MBA, EMBA, and other programs, covering tuition or living expenses.

- **Aga Khan Foundation Scholarship:** Offers postgraduate scholarships to exceptional students from developing countries, including those in France, who demonstrate strong academic records and leadership potential.

- **Campus France Scholarships:** Provides information on a range of scholarships for international students in France from various organizations (governments, universities, private foundations) across disciplines and degree levels.

- **Rhône-Alpes Scholarships:** Offered by the Rhône-Alpes region to international students pursuing higher education in the area's universities and institutions, designed to support academic excellence.

Required Documents:

Undergraduate Applications:

- Completed online application form.

- Official high school transcripts showing grades and courses.

- Copy of high school diploma or leaving certificate.

- Proof of language proficiency (French DELF/DALF or English TOEFL/IELTS, if applicable).

- Personal statement outlining academic interests and motivations.

- One or more letters of recommendation from teachers or counselors.

- Copy of passport or identification document.

- CV/Resume summarizing educational background and extracurricular activities.

- Application fee (if required).

Postgraduate Applications:

- Completed online application form.

- Official bachelor's degree transcripts showing grades and courses.

- Copy of bachelor's degree certificate.

- Proof of language proficiency in the language of instruction (French or English).

- Detailed Curriculum Vitae (CV) highlighting academic achievements and work experience.

- Statement of Purpose outlining academic and professional goals.

- Typically, two or three letters of recommendation from professors or professionals.

- Copy of passport or identification document.

- GRE/GMAT scores (if required by the program).

English-Taught Programs:

France offers various English-taught programs to help students improve their language proficiency while studying in an English-speaking environment and immersing in French culture. These include:

- University programs (Bachelor's, Master's, PhD) in fields like business, engineering, humanities, and social sciences (e.g., Sciences Po, INSEAD).

- Language schools and institutes offering intensive English language courses (e.g., Alliance Française, EF Education First).

- Summer language programs combine English language and culture with activities and excursions.

- TEFL/TESOL certification programs are available for those wanting to teach English as a foreign language in France.

- Exchange programs with institutions in English-speaking countries.

- Language immersion programs with host families and English language classes.

PR / Citizenship:

Acquiring French citizenship (French nationality) involves a legal process with specific eligibility criteria, including:

- **Birth in France:** Automatic citizenship if born in France to at least one French citizen parent.

- **Birth to French Parents Abroad:** Eligibility may exist if born abroad to French parents, with rules depending on factors like parents' nationality and birthplace.

Please note that the rules for citizenship can be complex and may depend on individual circumstances. It's recommended that official French government resources be consulted for the most up-to-date and detailed information.

Marriage to a French Citizen:

If you are married to a French citizen and have resided in France for a specific duration, you may be eligible for French citizenship. The required length of marriage and residency can vary.

Naturalization:

Naturalization is the process of applying for and acquiring French citizenship. The general requirements include:

- **Residence Requirement:** Legal residency in France for a specific period, typically five years (shorter for refugees or spouses of French citizens).

- **Integration:** Demonstrated commitment to French society through language proficiency, knowledge of French culture, and respect for French values.

- **Stable Income:** A steady source of income to support yourself and dependents.

- **No Criminal Record:** A clean criminal record.

- **Renunciation of Previous Citizenship:** Generally required, though exceptions exist if renunciation is impossible under your home country's laws.

Special Cases:

Additional pathways to citizenship exist for refugees, stateless persons, and individuals who have provided exceptional service to France.

Job Opportunities:

France offers a diverse job market across various sectors:

- **Information Technology (IT) and Tech Industries:** A growing sector, particularly in Paris and Lyon, with opportunities in software development, cybersecurity, data analysis, AI, and tech startups.

- **Engineering and Manufacturing:** A strong sector producing automobiles, aerospace products, and machinery, with roles for engineers, technicians, and production specialists.

- **Healthcare and Life Sciences:** Opportunities for doctors, nurses, researchers, pharmacists, and medical technology/biotechnology professionals.

- **Tourism and Hospitality:** A globally renowned industry with jobs in hospitality management, tourism promotion, hotel operations, and restaurant services.

- **Education and Research:** Prestigious universities and research institutions offer teaching and research positions for professors, researchers, and academic administrators.

- **Consulting and Professional Services:** Consulting firms offer services in management, strategy, and business functions, with roles for management consultants, business analysts, and financial advisors.

- **Fashion and Luxury Goods:** As a global fashion hub, France offers opportunities in design, marketing, retail, and production for renowned luxury brands.

- **Media and Entertainment:** Includes film, television, publishing, and advertising, with opportunities for journalists, editors, producers, and creative professionals.

- **Language Teaching:** Non-French speakers can find opportunities to teach their native language (e.g., English) in language schools and institutes.

The job market can be competitive, and French language skills are often crucial, especially for roles involving local interaction. Networking, company research, and understanding job requirements are vital. Expatriates should also consider the cost of living, work permits, and visa regulations.

Chapter 19

Studying in Hungary

Hungary offers a high-quality education system with a long tradition of academic excellence and numerous reputable universities. Many programs are in English, increasing accessibility for international students. Hungary also offers relatively affordable tuition for both EU and non-EU students compared to many Western European countries.

Hungarian universities provide diverse academic programs across arts and humanities, sciences, engineering, medicine, and business, with undergraduate, master's, and doctoral degrees available. Its central European location fosters interaction with diverse peers and provides a global perspective.

Hungary boasts a rich cultural heritage with historical landmarks, museums, and festivals, offering opportunities to explore European history and traditions. While Hungarian is the official language, English is widely spoken in urban areas, easing daily life for international students.

The country actively participates in international research collaborations, and Hungarian universities offer numerous research opportunities. As an EU member, Hungary provides easier access for EU students and convenient travel within the EU.

While studying in Hungary offers many advantages, researching specific universities and programs is crucial to finding the best fit for your academic and personal goals.

Top Ten Universities:

1. **Eötvös Loránd University (ELTE):** One of Hungary's oldest and most prestigious universities in Budapest, offering a wide range of programs.
2. **Central European University (CEU):** An international institution in Budapest and Vienna specializing in social sciences, humanities, and public policy, known for academic freedom and research.

3. **University of Debrecen:** A leading university in Debrecen, renowned for its medical and agricultural faculties.
4. **Budapest University of Technology and Economics (BME):** Hungary's oldest technical university in Budapest, offering engineering, technology, and natural sciences programs with a strong STEM reputation.
5. **University of Szeged:** Located in Szeged, known for research excellence and diverse academic programs with an emphasis on international collaboration.
6. **Semmelweis University:** In Budapest, renowned for medical and health sciences programs and one of Europe's oldest medical schools.
7. **Corvinus University of Budapest:** Known for its economics, business, and social sciences programs, it has a strong international focus.
8. **University of Pécs:** Located in Pécs, it offers diverse programs with a strong emphasis on research and internationalization.
9. **University of Miskolc:** Situated in Miskolc, specializing in engineering, technology, and natural sciences, known for industrial and technical research contributions.
10. **Budapest Business School (BBS):** A leading institution in Hungary for business and economics education in Budapest.

Entry Requirements:

Entry requirements vary by study level, university, program, and EU/non-EU status.

Undergraduate (Bachelor's) Programs:

- A high school diploma or equivalent is typically required. Specific requirements vary by program.
- English proficiency may need to be demonstrated via IELTS or TOEFL for English-taught programs. Some universities accept institution-issued certificates.

- Competitive programs (e.g., medicine, architecture) may require entrance exams or interviews.
- Completion of the university's application form and submission of required documents by the deadline is necessary.
- Copies of high school transcripts and certificates are required for verification.
- Non-EU students may need to show proof of sufficient financial resources.

Postgraduate (Master's and Doctoral) Programs:

- A relevant bachelor's degree (for Master's) or Master's degree (for Doctoral) is typically required.
- English proficiency may need to be demonstrated via IELTS or TOEFL for English-taught programs. Some universities offer language assessments.
- Some competitive programs may require entrance exams or interviews.
- Copies of academic transcripts and certificates from previous degrees are needed.
- Doctoral applicants may need to submit a research proposal.
- Letters of recommendation from professors or professionals are often required.
- Completion of the university's application form and adherence to deadlines are necessary.

It is crucial to check the specific requirements for your chosen program on the university's official website or contact their admissions office for detailed and up-to-date information. Non-EU students should also inquire about immigration and visa requirements.

Scholarships:

- **Stipendium Hungaricum Scholarship:** A fully funded scholarship by the Hungarian government for international students pursuing Bachelor's, Master's, and Doctoral programs, covering tuition, accommodation, and a monthly stipend.

- **Central European University (CEU) Scholarships:** Offers merit-based and need-based scholarships for international Master's and Doctoral students in social sciences, humanities, law, and public policy.
- **Erasmus+ Scholarships:** An EU-funded program that provides scholarships and grants for European and international students to study in Hungary and other European countries, supporting both short-term exchanges and full-degree programs.
- **Eötvös Loránd University (ELTE) Scholarships:** Offers several scholarships and tuition fee waivers for talented international students, including the ELTE Excellence Scholarship and ELTE Science and Innovation Scholarship.
- **Hungarian Scholarship Board Scholarships (MAB):** Provides scholarships to international students for Bachelor's, Master's, and Doctoral studies in Hungary, covering tuition fees and providing a stipend.
- **Visegrad Fund Scholarships:** Offers scholarships for students from Visegrad Group countries (Czech Republic, Hungary, Poland, Slovakia) to study in any of these countries, supporting Bachelor's, Master's, and Doctoral studies.
- **University-Specific Scholarships:** Many Hungarian universities offer their own scholarships and financial aid to international students based on academic excellence, specific programs, or diversity.
- **DAAD Scholarships:** The German Academic Exchange Service (DAAD) offers scholarships for German students to study in Hungary and vice versa, supporting various academic levels and fields.
- **Fulbright Scholarships:** Provides scholarships for U.S. citizens to conduct research, teach, or pursue graduate studies in Hungary, promoting academic and cultural exchange.

- **Scholarship Programs from Home Countries:** Various governments and organizations from other countries offer scholarships for their citizens to study in Hungary (e.g., Chinese Government Scholarships, Turkish Scholarships).

Required Documents:

- Ensure your passport is valid for your entire stay in Hungary with at least one blank visa page.
- Depending on your nationality, you may need a student visa to enter Hungary, and you may then need to apply for a student residence permit upon arrival. Consult the Hungarian embassy or consulate in your country for specific requirements.
- Letter of acceptance from the Hungarian university confirming your enrollment and program details.
- Proof of sufficient financial funds to cover tuition and living expenses (bank statements, scholarship letters, sponsorship documents).
- Proof of valid health insurance coverage in Hungary. Some universities may require a specific plan.
- Several passport-sized photos for visa, residence permit, and student ID applications.
- Copies of academic transcripts and certificates, including high school and previous degrees. Check for specific program requirements.
- Language proficiency test scores (IELTS, TOEFL, or others as required) if your program is not in your native language.
- Detailed CV or resume highlighting academic achievements, work experience, and extracurricular activities.
- Statement of purpose or motivation letter explaining your reasons for studying in Hungary, academic and career goals, and program alignment.
- Evidence of your accommodation in Hungary (housing contract or university dormitory confirmation).

- A copy of your birth certificate may be required.

PR / Citizenship:

- **EU/EEA Citizens:** Have the right to live and work in Hungary without a residence permit but may choose to apply for a Registration Certificate (Európai Unió Állampolgársága Bejelentése) to document their residence.
- **Non-EU/EEA Citizens (Permanent Residency):**
  - **Long-Term Visa:** Initially apply for a long-term visa for a specific purpose (work, study, family reunification, investment).
  - **Temporary Residence Permit:** Apply after arrival, typically valid for up to two years.
  - **Continuous Residence:** Maintain continuous legal residence during the temporary permit's validity.
  - **Permanent Residence Permit:** After residing legally for several years (usually five), you can apply for a permanent permit allowing indefinite stay.

Job Opportunities:

High-paying job opportunities in Hungary exist across various industries, with income depending on qualifications, experience, and the specific role.

- **Engineering:** Strong sector, especially in automotive and manufacturing. Well-compensated roles for mechanical, electrical, and software engineers.
- **Medical and Healthcare:** Competitive salaries for healthcare professionals, particularly doctors and specialists, in both public and private facilities.
- **Pharmaceuticals and Life Sciences:** Well-paying positions in the strong pharmaceutical industry for research, development, and production professionals.
- **Real Estate and Property Management:** Significant income potential for agents, property managers, and developers, especially in active urban centers.

- **Consulting:** Lucrative careers for management, IT, and other specialized consultants providing expertise to businesses.

Salary levels vary based on qualifications, experience, location, and employer. Hungary's lower cost of living compared to many Western European countries can increase the purchasing power of higher salaries.

Chapter 20

Studying in China

Studying abroad in China offers significant academic and personal advantages. Its rich and diverse culture provides a unique immersion in language, traditions, and history, fostering personal growth and global awareness.

Learning Mandarin, a widely spoken global language can greatly enhance language skills and career prospects as China's global influence expands.

China has invested heavily in its higher education system, with several universities ranking among the world's best. Many offer English-taught programs, increasing accessibility for international students.

Compared to Western countries, China offers more affordable tuition and lower living costs, making it attractive for cost-effective, high-quality education. It's also a growing global hub for research and innovation, particularly in technology, engineering, and science, with cutting-edge facilities and international collaborations.

China's rapidly growing economy presents numerous internship and job opportunities, especially for those proficient in Mandarin. Companies increasingly seek internationally educated graduates with a global perspective, making China an excellent place for building connections and gaining professional experience.

Top Ten Universities:

1. **Peking University (PKU):** In Beijing, one of China's oldest and most prestigious, known for humanities, sciences, and social sciences.

2. **Tsinghua University:** Also in Beijing, renowned for engineering, computer science, and technology programs, consistently ranked globally.

3. **Fudan University:** Located in Shanghai, known for excellence in social sciences, business, and economics with a strong international reputation.

4. **Zhejiang University:** In Hangzhou, recognized for science and engineering research, part of China's "Double First Class" initiative.

5. **Shanghai Jiao Tong University (SJTU):** In Shanghai, well-regarded for engineering and business programs, home to the Shanghai Ranking.

6. **University of Science and Technology of China (USTC):** In Hefei, a top research university focused on science and technology, known for scientific advancements.

7. **Nanjing University:** Nanjing is a comprehensive institution known for the humanities, natural sciences, and social sciences.

8. **Sun Yat-sen University:** Guangzhou is known for its medical and business schools, and it is a key player in China's education.

9. **Harbin Institute of Technology (HIT):** Harbin is renowned for its engineering and technical programs, producing skilled engineers and innovators.

10. **Wuhan University:** Wuhan, known for its strengths in medicine, engineering, and humanities, is one of China's oldest and most prestigious.

Entry Requirements:

1. **Language Proficiency:** For Chinese-taught programs, you'll typically need to demonstrate Mandarin proficiency through the HSK (Hanyu Shuiping Kaoshi) exam. Different programs and universities have varying HSK score requirements, so check specific program details.

2. **Academic Qualifications:**

   o **Undergraduate:** High school diploma or equivalent. Specific requirements vary by university and program.

   o **Postgraduate:** Bachelor's degree or equivalent relevant to your intended field of study.

3. **Entrance Examinations:** Some universities and programs, especially competitive ones or those offering scholarships, may require additional entrance exams, including subject-specific tests or interviews.

Selecting the Right Program:

- **Define Goals:** Determine your academic and career goals (field of study, degree level, research interests, professional development).

- **Language Preference:** Decide whether you prefer studying in English or Mandarin, as this will narrow your program options.

- **University Research:** Look for universities in China offering programs in your field of interest, starting with top universities and considering other reputable institutions.

- **Accreditation:** Ensure that your chosen universities and programs are accredited by relevant Chinese authorities.

- **Program Details:** Review course curriculum, faculty, research opportunities, and special features on university websites to see if the program aligns with your interests and goals.

- **Location Preference:** Consider your preferred location in China, thinking about climate, urban vs. rural settings, and proximity to major cities.

- **Admission Requirements:** Check and ensure you meet the prerequisites for academic and language proficiency. Some programs may require standardized tests like GRE or GMAT.

- **Financial Planning:** Calculate the total cost of studying in China (tuition, living expenses, miscellaneous charges) and research scholarship and financial aid options.

Top Ten Scholarships:

1. **Chinese Government Scholarship (CSC):** Prestigious, fully funded scholarship covering tuition, accommodation, and a monthly stipend for undergraduate, Master's, and Doctoral students.

2. **Confucius Institute Scholarship:** Sponsored by Hanban, supports international students studying the Chinese language and culture, including tuition, accommodation, and a living allowance.

3. **Chinese University Scholarships:** Many universities offer their own scholarships with varying eligibility, coverage, and application procedures. Check specific university details.

4. **Silk Road Scholarship:** Initiated by China's Ministry of Education to promote educational cooperation along Silk Road countries, supporting degrees related to the Belt and Road Initiative.

5. **Great Wall Program (MOFCOM Scholarship):** Supports students from developing countries pursuing a Master's degree in economics, management, and related fields.

6. **Jiangsu Jasmine Scholarship:** Offered by the Jiangsu Provincial Government for international students at all levels, providing full or partial tuition and a living allowance.

7. **Shanghai Government Scholarship:** Supports international students in Shanghai, covering tuition and providing a monthly stipend.

8. **Zhejiang University Scholarship:** Offers various scholarships for international students, including the Outstanding International Students Scholarship, covering tuition and providing a living allowance.

9. **Beijing Government Scholarship:** This scholarship is available for international students pursuing degree programs in Beijing, covering tuition, accommodation, and a monthly living allowance.

10. **Tianjin Government Scholarship:** Supports international students studying in Tianjin, covering tuition and providing a monthly living allowance.

Documentation:

- **Application Form:** Complete the university's application form, usually found on their official website, with some universities offering online systems.

- **Academic Records:**

  - **Undergraduate:** High school transcripts or academic records detailing courses, grades, and graduation dates.

  - **Postgraduate:** Bachelor's degree transcripts and certificates. If applicable, Master's degree transcripts and certificates.

- **Language Proficiency Test Scores:**

  - **Chinese-taught programs:** HSK (Hanyu Shuiping Kaoshi) scores to demonstrate Mandarin proficiency.

  - **English-taught programs:** IELTS or TOEFL scores to demonstrate English proficiency.

- **Letter(s) of Recommendation:** Typically, one or more letters from teachers, professors, or professionals attest to your academic abilities and potential.

- **Statement of Purpose (SOP) or Personal Statement:** A written statement outlining your academic and career goals, interest in the program, and its alignment with your aspirations.

- **Passport Copy:** A clear copy of your passport's biographical page, ensuring its validity throughout your intended stay in China.

- **Health Examination Report:** Many universities require a medical examination in your home country, with the report submitted as part of the application to ensure good health upon arrival.

- **Financial Documents:** Proof of your ability to cover education and living expenses, such as bank statements, scholarship awards, or financial guarantee letters.

PR / Citizenship:

1. **Chinese Citizenship:** Generally challenging for foreign nationals due to strict rules against dual citizenship, requiring renunciation of other citizenships. Common pathways include:

   - **Marriage to a Chinese Citizen:** Eligibility after a specified period of residence in China (usually at least five years), with requirements varying by local authorities.

   - **Birthright:** Children born in China to at least one Chinese parent are typically considered Chinese citizens, regardless of the other parent's nationality.

   - **Naturalization:** Possible in some cases with stringent requirements, including a substantial residency period and contributions to China.

2. **Permanent Residency (PR) in China:** A more feasible option for foreign nationals ("Chinese Green Card"). General eligibility and application process:

   - **Eligibility Criteria:** Stable income or employment, significant contributions to China, and meeting specific requirements set by the Public Security Bureau (PSB).

   - **Application Documents:** Valid passport, residence permit, health examination reports, criminal record check, proof of income or assets, and other supporting documents.

   - **Application Procedure:** Submission to the local PSB or the Entry and Exit Administration of the PSB, potentially followed by an interview or investigation.

- **Decision:** Review by the PSB; if approved, a Chinese Green Card is issued, allowing you to live and work in China without needing a work or residence permit.

Job Opportunities:

China offers a range of high-paying job opportunities across various industries, with specific salaries varying based on qualifications, experience, location, and sector.

Chapter 21

Studying in Ireland

Ireland is known for its excellent, globally recognized education system with prestigious universities and colleges. For non-native English speakers, studying in Ireland significantly enhances language skills, which is a valuable career asset.

Living and studying in Ireland offers full immersion in Irish culture, allowing interaction with locals, learning traditions, and exploring rich history and heritage.

Beyond academics, Ireland's breathtaking landscapes offer exploration opportunities. As a popular international student destination, it provides a chance to build a global network and gain diverse perspectives.

With a strong economy, Ireland allows many international students to work part-time during studies and full-time during breaks, aiding finances and providing work experience. Attractive post-study work opportunities like the Third Level Graduate Scheme allow graduates to stay and work for a specified period.

Top 10 Universities:

1. **Trinity College Dublin (TCD):** One of Ireland's oldest and most prestigious, renowned for academic excellence and its historic Dublin campus, consistently ranking among top global universities.

2. **University College Dublin (UCD):** Ireland's largest university, known for strong research and innovation, offering diverse programs and a vibrant campus community.

3. **University College Cork (UCC):** A research-intensive institution in Cork known for strong science, technology, and healthcare programs, a beautiful campus, and a commitment to sustainability.

4. **National University of Ireland, Galway (NUIG):** Situated in Galway, it is known for its research excellence, particularly in medicine, science, and technology.

5. **Dublin City University (DCU):** A young and dynamic Dublin university recognized for innovative teaching and strong industry links, fostering entrepreneurship.

6. **University of Limerick (UL):** Known for its modern campus and strong emphasis on cooperative education, excelling in engineering, business, and related fields.

7. **Maynooth University:** Located outside Dublin, offering a wide range of programs with a strong focus on humanities and social sciences, a vibrant campus, and a close-knit community.

8. **Technological University Dublin (TU Dublin) (formerly Dublin Institute of Technology - DIT):** Known for prominent programs in engineering, architecture, business, and creative arts, playing a significant role in Dublin's education.

9. **University of Dublin, Royal College of Surgeons in Ireland (RCSI):** A specialized medical university in Dublin, internationally recognized for its medical and healthcare programs, including surgery and pharmacy.

10. **Dublin Business School (DBS):** A leading institution for business and management studies in Ireland, offering a wide range of programs and a strong reputation for employability.

Entry Requirements:

- **Academic Qualifications:** High school diploma (undergraduate) or relevant bachelor's degree (postgraduate).

- **English Language Proficiency:** IELTS or TOEFL scores if your primary language isn't English. Minimum scores vary by university.

- **Program-Specific Requirements:** Additional criteria for some programs (e.g., specific academic background, work experience, portfolios).

- **Entrance Examinations:** Some programs (e.g., medicine, dentistry) may require exams like HPAT or GAMSAT.

- **Reference Letters and Personal Statements:** Letters from teachers/professors and a statement explaining your motivations and goals.

- **Visa Requirements:** Non-EU/EEA students may need a student visa. Check the Irish government's official website or the Irish embassy/consulate in your home country.

- **Financial Proof:** Demonstration of sufficient funds for tuition and living expenses, often required for visa applications.

Scholarships and Funding:

- **Government of Ireland Scholarships for International Students:** For high-achieving non-EU/EEA postgraduate students, covering tuition, stipend, and allowances.

- **Irish Research Council Scholarships:** For postgraduate research in various fields, supporting Irish and international students.

- **Trinity College Dublin Scholarships:** Merit-based scholarships for international undergraduate and postgraduate students.

- **University College Dublin (UCD) Global Excellence Scholarships:** For high-achieving international students in full-time undergraduate or postgraduate programs, covering a portion of tuition.

- **University College Cork (UCC) Scholarships:** For international undergraduate and postgraduate students, typically based on academic excellence or program-specific criteria.

- **Government of Ireland International Education Scholarships:** Administered by Irish higher education institutions for non-EU/EEA students in undergraduate and postgraduate programs, covering a portion of tuition.

- **Maynooth University Scholarships:** Merit-based international scholarships for undergraduate and postgraduate students.

- **Dublin City University (DCU) Scholarships:** Various scholarships for international students, including merit-based awards.

- **University of Limerick Scholarships:** Selection of scholarships for undergraduate and postgraduate students based on academic excellence, leadership, or other criteria.

- **Fulbright Awards:** For U.S. and Irish citizens to study, research, or teach in each other's countries, promoting cultural exchange and academic collaboration.

Required Documents:

- **Application Form:** Complete the online form from the university or college.

- **Academic Transcripts:** Official records from previous educational institutions.

- **Proof of English Proficiency:** IELTS or TOEFL scores (if applicable).

- **Curriculum Vitae (CV) or Resume:** Detailing your educational background, work experience, and achievements.

- **Personal Statement or Statement of Purpose:** Explaining your motivations and goals.

- **Letters of Recommendation:** From teachers, professors, or employers.

- **Passport Copy:** Valid for the duration of your studies.

- **Proof of Funding:** Demonstrating sufficient financial resources.

- **Visa Documentation:** These are the required documents for your student visa application (if applicable).

- **Application Fee:** Payment as specified by the institution.

PR / Citizenship:

- **Post-Study Work Visas:**

  - **Graduate Route:** Allows international graduates (undergraduate level or above) to stay and work for up to 24 months post-graduation.

  - **Doctorate Extension Scheme:** PhD students can extend their stay for up to 24 months after completing studies to seek employment or start a business.

- **General Work Visas:** Can be applied for after completing a post-study work visa.

- **Critical Skills Employment Permit:** For jobs in the Critical Skills Occupations list, leading to PR after two years of employment.

- **Stamp 4 Permission:** May be eligible after five years of living in Ireland on various immigration permissions, allowing unrestricted work and life.

- **Permanent Residency (PR):** This can be applied for after five years of Stamp 4 permission.

- **Irish Citizenship:** May be eligible after five years of PR (including time spent on other eligible visas).

Job Opportunities:

Ireland's job market is growing, offering high-salary opportunities in technology, **healthcare, finance, engineering, legal and law, aviation, consulting, and pharmaceuticals.**

It's important to note that salary levels can vary depending on location (e.g., Dublin generally has higher salaries), years of experience, qualifications, and the specific company or organization. Additionally, the cost of living in Ireland, particularly in major cities like Dublin, can be relatively high, so salary levels often reflect this.

Chapter 22

Studying in New Zealand

Studying abroad in New Zealand offers numerous benefits, starting with its **high-quality education system**. The country boasts world-renowned universities that consistently rank well globally, offering a wide array of programs.

New Zealand is known for its **welcoming and inclusive society**, providing a multicultural environment that fosters cross-cultural understanding and enhances interpersonal skills.

The country's **natural beauty and outdoor recreational opportunities** are another significant advantage, with stunning landscapes offering activities like hiking, skiing, and water sports.

New Zealand has a strong emphasis on **research and innovation**, making it ideal for STEM students with vibrant research communities and cutting-edge facilities.

The **New Zealand government offers various scholarships and financial aid** for international students, making education more accessible and affordable, with a relatively reasonable cost of living.

New Zealand provides a favorable environment for post-graduation opportunities, allowing graduates to apply for post-study work visas to gain valuable work experience.

Top Universities in New Zealand:

1. **University of Auckland:** New Zealand's largest and most prestigious university, consistently ranked among the top 100 globally, is known for its research-oriented environment and many programs.

2. **University of Otago:** Located in Dunedin, renowned for excellence in research and teaching, particularly in health sciences, humanities, and natural sciences, with a rich history and outstanding reputation.

3. **University of Canterbury:** Known for its picturesque Christchurch campus, which excels in engineering, science, and technology, it is a hub for innovation and research.

4. **Victoria University of Wellington:** In the capital city, esteemed for its social sciences, humanities, and business programs, offering a vibrant and diverse academic environment.

5. **University of Waikato:** Located in Hamilton, it is known for its strong focus on research and innovation, especially in agriculture, environmental science, and computer science.

6. **Massey University:** New Zealand's leading institution for agriculture, veterinary science, and related disciplines, with multiple campuses across the country.

7. **Lincoln University:** A top choice for those interested in the agri-food sector, specializing in agriculture, agribusiness, and related fields, with a strong emphasis on sustainability and environmental science.

8. **AUT University (Auckland University of Technology):** Known for its modern, practical, and industry-relevant programs, popular for business, technology, and creative arts.

9. **University of Waikato:** Located in Hamilton, it is known for its strong focus on research and innovation, especially in agriculture, environmental science, and computer science.

10. **University of Otago:** Situated in Dunedin, renowned for its excellence in research and teaching, particularly shining in health sciences, humanities, and natural sciences, with a rich history and strong international reputation.

Entry Requirements

University entry requirements in New Zealand can vary depending on the specific institution and program you are interested in. However, some general guidelines and standard requirements apply to most universities.

Academic Qualifications:

High School Diploma: For undergraduate programs, international students must have completed their secondary education, equivalent to New Zealand's National Certificate of Educational Achievement (NCEA) Level 3 or another recognized qualification.

Bachelor's Degree: For admission to postgraduate programs, you must have completed a relevant bachelor's degree or equivalent. Some programs may require a specific minimum GPA or academic standing.

English Language Proficiency:

English Proficiency Test: Most universities require international students to demonstrate their English language proficiency. Commonly accepted tests include IELTS, TOEFL, or PTE Academic. The required scores can vary but generally fall in the IELTS 6.0-7.0 range, TOEFL iBT 80-100, or PTE Academic 58-65 for undergraduate programs, and higher scores for postgraduate programs.

Waivers: Some universities may waive the English language requirement if your previous education was conducted in English or if you can provide evidence of sufficient proficiency through other means.

Finding the Right Program

To find the right program in New Zealand, thoughtfully align your academic and career goals with available options. Begin by identifying your field of interest and long-term aspirations, which will direct your search among New Zealand's diverse universities and institutions renowned in various fields. Consider their reputation, location, and facilities. Your preferred study location within New Zealand also matters as cities like Auckland offer extensive programs, while others provide a different atmosphere. Explore university websites, noting specific courses and specializations. Review admission prerequisites, including academic and English language requirements, as well as program duration and structure (undergraduate, postgraduate, research-based, etc.). Factor in tuition fees and investigate potential scholarships from universities, government bodies, and other organizations. Seek guidance from academic advisors and connect with alumni or current students for firsthand insights. Finally, consider your lifestyle preferences and engage in education fairs or webinars to gather more information and ask questions.

Scholarships and Funding

New Zealand Government Scholarships: These prestigious, government-funded scholarships support international students across all study levels (undergraduate, postgraduate, doctoral), covering tuition, living costs, and other expenses.

Fulbright New Zealand Scholarships: Administered by Fulbright New Zealand, these scholarships facilitate academic and cultural exchanges between New Zealand and the U.S., offering opportunities for study or research in either country.

University of Auckland Scholarships: This university provides diverse scholarships for domestic and international students, often merit-based and spanning various fields and academic levels.

University of Otago Scholarships: Otago offers numerous scholarships for international students in undergraduate and postgraduate programs, assisting with tuition and living expenses.

Victoria University of Wellington Scholarships: Wellington provides various scholarships, including the Wellington International Excellence Scholarship for high-achieving international students.

University of Canterbury Scholarships: Canterbury offers several scholarships for international students, such as the UC International First Year Scholarship and UC International College Scholarships.

Massey University Scholarships: Massey University provides scholarships for international students at different study levels, helping with tuition and other costs.

Lincoln University Scholarships: Lincoln University offers scholarships for international students in undergraduate, postgraduate, or doctoral programs, particularly in agriculture, environmental science, and related areas.

AUT Scholarships (Auckland University of Technology): AUT supports international students in undergraduate and postgraduate business, health sciences, and creative arts programs through its scholarships.

Education New Zealand Scholarships: Education New Zealand offers various scholarships, including the New Zealand Excellence Awards and New Zealand ASEAN Scholar Awards, fostering educational links between New Zealand and specific regions.

Documentation

Start by completing the university's online or paper application forms if available. This form serves as the initial step in the application process.

Academic Transcripts:

Submit certified copies of your academic transcripts and certificates from your previous educational institutions. These documents should provide details of your academic performance and qualifications.

Proof of English Language Proficiency:

If English is not your native language, you will typically need to provide proof of English language proficiency through standardized tests such as IELTS, TOEFL, or PTE Academic. Ensure that your scores meet the specific requirements of the university and program you're applying to.

Personal Statement:

Write a statement of purpose (SOP) or personal statement explaining your academic and career goals, why you want to study in New Zealand, and your interest in the specific program.

Passport Copy:

Provide a certified copy of your passport, including your personal information, photograph, and passport number. Ensure that your passport is valid for your intended stay in New Zealand.

Proof of Funds:

Demonstrate your ability to cover tuition fees and living expenses in New Zealand. This may include bank statements, financial guarantee letters, or scholarship award letters.

Visa and Immigration Documents:

Be prepared to provide documents related to your visa application, including visa application forms, health and character certificates, and any other documents required by the New Zealand Immigration Service.

Application Fee:

Many universities in New Zealand charge an application fee. Ensure that you pay this fee as part of your application process. Keep copies of payment receipts as proof.

Translations and Notarization:

You may need to provide certified translations if your documents are not in English. Additionally, some universities may require notarized copies of your documents.

PR/Citizenship

New Zealand offers several pathways for international students seeking permanent residency (PR) or citizenship post graduation.

1. **Post-Study Work Visa (Open):** Completing studies may qualify you for a Post-Study Work Visa (Open), allowing you to work in New Zealand for up to 12 months to explore job opportunities related to your field, potentially leading to long-term employment.

2. **Post-Study Employer-Assisted Work Visa:** If you secure a job relevant to your qualifications and your employer supports your application, you can apply for this visa, typically granted for 2-3 years, offering valuable work experience.

3. **Skilled Migrant Category (SMC) Visa:** New Zealand's points-based SMC visa considers factors like age, work experience, qualifications, and job offers. Meeting the required points can lead to permanent residency.

4. **Long-Term Skill Shortage List (LTSSL) Work Visa:** If your occupation is on the LTSSL and you have a job offer in that field, you may be eligible for a work visa. Work experience gained through this visa can contribute to PR eligibility.

5. **Residence from Work Visa:** After a specified period of working in New Zealand on a work visa, you may be eligible to apply for a Residence from Work Visa, potentially leading to permanent residency if requirements are met.

6. **Partner or Family Sponsorship:** A New Zealand citizen, permanent resident partner, or family member may sponsor your visa application, which can lead to permanent residency.

7. **Citizenship:** After obtaining permanent residency and meeting specific criteria, you can apply for New Zealand citizenship, granting full rights and the ability to live in the country indefinitely.

It's crucial to note that visa requirements and eligibility can change. Consult the New Zealand Immigration Service (INZ) or an immigration advisor for the most current and personalized information.

Job Opportunities

Job opportunities in New Zealand span various sectors for skilled individuals and recent graduates; those with degrees in in-demand fields like **engineering, healthcare, information technology,**

agriculture, and **education** may qualify for skilled employment and potential work visas or permanent residency, while post-study work visas allow international graduates to gain valuable work experience after their studies, with some companies offering structured graduate programs in areas such as **finance**, **engineering**, and **consulting**; advanced degree holders can pursue opportunities in **research and academia**, and the growing **healthcare** sector consistently seeks doctors, nurses, and allied health workers; **agriculture** offers roles in agricultural science, horticulture, and viticulture, alongside seasonal work; the thriving **tourism and hospitality** industry provides jobs in hotels, restaurants, and related businesses; the expanding **information technology** sector needs software developers, system administrators, and cybersecurity experts; talented individuals can find opportunities in the **creative industries**, including film, animation, design, and music; infrastructure development creates demand in **engineering and construction** for engineers, architects, and construction professionals; the **business and finance** sector offers roles in finance, accounting, marketing, and management; and with a focus on conservation, the **environmental and sustainability** sector presents opportunities for graduates in related fields; researching the job market and networking are crucial for finding suitable employment.

Chapter 23

Studying in Japan

Studying abroad in Japan presents numerous compelling advantages for international students. Japan boasts a world-class education system featuring top-ranking universities with cutting-edge facilities, experienced faculty, and a rigorous academic environment that enhances educational and career prospects.

Immersing oneself in Japan's rich and unique culture is another significant draw. The country's deep-rooted traditions, vibrant festivals, and daily life offer firsthand cultural experiences, broadening perspectives and fostering adaptability.

Japan is also renowned for its safety and low crime rates, providing a secure environment for international students. Its efficient public transportation and infrastructure facilitate easy exploration of diverse landscapes, from bustling cities to serene rural areas.

Language acquisition is a valuable benefit. While many courses are in English, the opportunity to learn or improve Japanese skills is invaluable, opening doors to diverse job opportunities both in Japan and internationally, particularly in technology, finance, and business.

As a global economic powerhouse with prominent corporations and innovative startups, Japan offers networking and internship opportunities, enhancing future employment prospects. The Japanese work ethic and business culture provide valuable, sought-after skills.

Beyond academics and career benefits, studying in Japan fosters lifelong international friendships. The country's welcoming atmosphere and rich heritage make it easy to connect with locals and fellow international students, creating a diverse and supportive community.

Top 10 Universities:

- **University of Tokyo (Todai):** Japan's oldest and most prestigious institution, consistently ranking globally, offering diverse academic programs.

- **Kyoto University:** Renowned for research and education excellence, particularly in science, engineering, and humanities, with a history of Nobel laureates.

- **Osaka University:** Known for its strong emphasis on innovation and research, a leader in science and technology.

- **Tokyo Institute of Technology (Tokyo Tech):** A top-tier institution specializing in rigorous science and engineering programs and technological advancements.

- **Tohoku University:** In Sendai, recognized for research in natural sciences, medicine, and engineering, with a strong international presence.

- **Nagoya University:** Recognized for comprehensive academics and contributions to physics, chemistry, and social sciences research, with a commitment to internationalization.

- **Kyushu University:** In Fukuoka, known for its global outlook and research initiatives, offering diverse programs and emphasizing international partnerships.

- **Hokkaido University:** In Sapporo, a prominent research institution excelling in agriculture, environmental science, and engineering, promoting interdisciplinary research.

- **Keio University:** A leading private institution with a strong focus on liberal arts, offering programs including business, law, and social sciences, known for its global network.

- **Waseda University:** Another prestigious private university offering diverse programs in humanities, social sciences, and business, with a strong emphasis on internationalization and research.

Entry Requirements

University entry requirements in Japan can vary depending on the institution, degree program, and whether you are applying as a domestic or international student. Here are some general guidelines for university entry requirements in Japan:

High School Diploma or Equivalent:

For undergraduate programs, Japanese universities typically require applicants to complete their high school education or equivalent. This is the minimum educational qualification for admission.

Language Proficiency:

If you are an international student and your chosen program is taught in Japanese, you may need to demonstrate your Japanese language proficiency. This is usually done through standardized tests like the Japanese Language Proficiency Test (JLPT) or the Japanese University Admission for International Students (EJU) Examination.

Entrance Examinations:

Entrance examinations are a significant part of the admission process in Japan. Most Japanese universities, especially prestigious ones, require applicants to take standardized entrance exams specific to the university or the department they are applying to. These exams typically include subjects related to the chosen field of study.

Academic Transcripts:

You will need to provide your high school transcripts or academic records as part of your application. These transcripts should show your academic performance during your high school years.

Finding the Right Program

To find the right program at a Japanese university, begin by clearly understanding your academic and career goals. Define your passions and long-term aspirations to identify subjects or fields that resonate with you, forming the basis for your program selection.

Thoroughly research Japanese universities offering programs in your chosen field. Consider the university's reputation, location, campus facilities, and relevant resources to find a good academic fit.

Language of instruction is crucial. Determine if you prefer English or Japanese instruction, ensuring it aligns with your language skills for academic success.

Explore the specifics of each program's curriculum, courses, and specializations to match your academic interests and career goals.

Verify that you meet the academic and language proficiency admission requirements, including any standardized tests, recommendation letters, or interviews.

Consider the university's location, evaluating the cost of living, climate, proximity to cities or industry hubs, and cultural attractions for your well-being.

Check the total cost of education, including tuition, fees, and living expenses. Research available scholarships, grants, and financial aid for international students and create a budget.

Ensure the university and program are accredited and recognized by investigating rankings and academic reputation to gauge educational quality.

Reach out to current or former students for insights into the academic environment, faculty, and student life to inform your decision.

Participate in university information sessions and education fairs (in person or online) to interact with representatives and gather program and admission details.

Seek guidance from academic advisors or counselors for expert advice on program selection, application processes, and scholarships to navigate the complexities of choosing the right Japanese university program.

Scholarships

Japanese Government (MEXT) Scholarships: Prestigious scholarships for undergraduate, graduate, and research programs, covering tuition, living expenses, and round-trip airfare.

JASSO Scholarships (Monbukagakusho Honors Scholarship for Privately-Financed International Students): Provided by the Japan Student Services Organization (JASSO) based on academic achievement, helping with tuition and living costs for privately financed students.

Asian Development Bank-Japan Scholarship Program: Administered by the ADB, supporting postgraduate studies in Japan for students from ADB member countries, covering tuition, living expenses, and other educational costs.

Rotary Peace Fellowships: For individuals pursuing master's degrees or professional development certificates in peace and conflict resolution, providing funding for tuition, living expenses, and travel.

JSPS Postdoctoral Fellowships: Offered by the Japan Society for the Promotion of Science (JSPS) for researchers worldwide to support research at Japanese universities and institutions.

Toyota Foundation Research Grants: Supporting projects that contribute to societal and cultural advancement in Japan and other Asian countries.

Yamaha Music Foundation Scholarships: For outstanding music students pursuing degrees or diplomas in music-related fields in Japan, providing financial support for tuition and living expenses.

Nitori International Scholarship Foundation: Supports international undergraduate and graduate students studying in Japan based on academic performance and financial need.

Japan-IMF Scholarship Program for Advanced Studies: Sponsored by the IMF for students from selected Asian countries pursuing graduate studies in economics or related fields in Japan.

Kobe University Graduate School Scholarships for International Students: Offers various scholarships for international graduate students to help cover tuition and living expenses.

Documentation

Application Form:

Most universities in Japan provide an online application form that you must complete. This form typically includes personal information, educational history, and program preferences.

Academic Transcripts:

You will need to provide official transcripts from your previous educational institutions, such as high school or undergraduate institutions. These transcripts should detail your academic performance, courses taken, and grades earned.

Diploma or Degree Certificate:

Depending on the program level you are applying to (undergraduate, graduate, or doctoral), you may need to submit a copy of your high school diploma, bachelor's degree certificate, or equivalent documentation.

Language Proficiency Test Scores:

If you are applying for a program taught in Japanese and your native language is not Japanese, you may need to provide language proficiency test scores. The most commonly accepted tests are the Japanese Language Proficiency Test (JLPT) and the Japanese University Admission for International Students (EJU) Examination If applying for an English-taught program, you may need to provide scores for tests like TOEFL or IELTS.

Standardized Test Scores:

Some universities may require standardized test scores, such as the SAT or ACT for undergraduate programs or the GRE or GMAT for graduate programs. Check the specific program's admission requirements.

Letters of Recommendation:

Many universities request letters of recommendation from teachers, professors, or professionals who can attest to your academic abilities and character. Ensure you follow the university's guidelines regarding the number of letters required and submission procedures.

Statement of Purpose or Personal Statement:

Prepare a well-written statement of purpose or personal statement that explains your academic and career goals, why you are interested in the program, and how it aligns with your aspirations.

Passport Copy:

A copy of your passport's photo page may be required for identification purposes.

Photographs:

Some universities may request passport-sized photographs for administrative purposes. Check the university's guidelines for photo specifications.

Financial Documentation (for Visa Application):

To obtain a student visa, you will need to provide proof of sufficient funds to cover your tuition fees and living expenses in Japan. This may include bank statements, scholarship award letters, or financial affidavits.

PR / Citizenship

1. **Post-Study Work Visa (Designated Activities Visa):** After graduation, you can apply for the Designated Activities Visa, allowing up to one year in Japan to seek employment. Securing a job enables the transition to a work visa.

2. **Work Visas:** Upon employment, you can switch to a work visa (e.g., Engineer/Specialist in Humanities/International Services, Instructor, Skilled Labor), a common pathway for long-term stay tied to specific job roles.

3. **Highly Skilled Professional Visa:** This visa attracts highly skilled foreign professionals, with points awarded for education, experience, and income. Achieving a threshold can lead to preferential immigration treatment and a shorter PR application period.

4. **Permanent Residency (PR):** Requires meeting specific criteria, typically including a certain number of years of residence (usually ten, but potentially shorter for HSP visa holders). PR allows indefinite living and working in Japan without employment or location restrictions.

5. **Naturalization (Citizenship):** Possible but challenging, requiring at least five years of residency, good conduct, financial stability, willingness to renounce other citizenships, and passing a Japanese language test and interview. Japan does not allow dual citizenship.

Japan has strict immigration policies. Meeting minimum stay and eligibility is necessary at each stage. Naturalization can be demanding.

To improve your chances:

- Maintain an excellent academic and professional record.

- Learn Japanese, often required for PR and citizenship.

- Abide by Japanese immigration laws.

- Seek legal advice for visa or PR applications.

Japan welcomes skilled professionals, but careful navigation of the immigration process and understanding specific requirements are crucial for achieving your immigration goals.

Job Opportunities

Job opportunities in Japan are diverse and available for both citizens and international residents across various industries; the

technology and IT sector, home to global giants and a growing startup scene, offers roles in software development, data analysis, network engineering, and cybersecurity; the strong **manufacturing and engineering** sector, known for automotive, electronics, machinery, and robotics, has openings in mechanical and electrical engineering, quality control, production management, and R&D; Tokyo, a major financial hub, provides numerous **finance and banking** opportunities, including financial analysts, investment bankers, and asset managers; the aging population drives demand in **healthcare and pharmaceuticals** for doctors, nurses, pharmacists, and medical researchers; **education and language teaching**, particularly English through programs like JET, is a popular option for expatriates, alongside teaching other subjects; the growing **tourism and hospitality** industry offers jobs in hotels, restaurants, and travel agencies, where bilingualism is advantageous; **retail and sales** positions are abundant, from sales associates to management; **consulting and business services** firms seek experts in management, finance, and IT; bilingual individuals can work in **translation and interpretation**; the **creative and entertainment** industries offer roles in advertising, film, design, animation, and video games; a vital **research and academia** community provides positions at universities and research institutions; **agriculture and the food industry** include farming, food production, food safety, and culinary roles; the focus on sustainability creates opportunities in **environmental and renewable energy**; and the **government and public sector** offer administrative, policy, and diplomatic positions; however, Japanese language proficiency is often crucial for professional roles.

Chapter 24

Studying in India

India, with its rich cultural tapestry and as the origin of major world religions, offers compelling educational opportunities for international students. While studying in this captivating country might initially seem challenging, it can provide unique perspectives and experiences. Despite potential adjustments, India offers a rewarding and affordable study abroad experience with a fresh outlook.

India's appeal lies in its vibrant traditions, dynamic cities, and rapidly expanding economy. Its extensive education system includes numerous top-ranking universities, evidenced by the 41 Indian universities among the 1,422 listed in the 2023 QS World University Rankings, with seven new additions highlighting the sector's growth. Considering its offerings, India presents significant learning and personal growth, making it a strong choice for a transformative educational journey.

Top 10 Universities:

1. **Indian Institute of Science, Bangalore:** A government-recognized research university focused on higher education and research in science, engineering, design, and management.

2. **Indian Institute of Technology, Bombay:** A renowned public research university and technical institute in Mumbai, Maharashtra, a top choice for STEM fields.

3. **Indian Institute of Technology, Kharagpur:** The first IIT, established by the Government of India in West Bengal, is recognized as an Institute of National Importance for Technology and Research.

4. **Indian Institute of Technology, Madras:** A distinguished public technical university in Chennai, Tamil Nadu, selected as one of India's Institutes of Eminence.

5. **Indian Institute of Technology, Delhi:** A prominent Center of Excellence among the IITs for training, research, and development in science, engineering, and technology.

6. **University of Delhi:** A central university in Delhi, founded in 1922, holding the status of an Institute of Eminence.

7. **All India Institute of Medical Sciences, New Delhi:** A public medical research university and hospital operating autonomously under the Ministry of Health and Family Welfare.

8. **Indian Institute of Technology, Kanpur:** A notable public institute of technology in Uttar Pradesh, declared an Institute of National Importance.

9. **Jadavpur University, Kolkata:** A public state university, initially established as Bengal Technical Institute, ranking highly among Indian universities for its academic performance.

10. **Jawaharlal Nehru University:** A major public research university in New Delhi, renowned for its faculties and research focus on social and applied sciences.

Entry Requirements

All international students, excluding those from the United Kingdom, must fulfill our English language requirements. If you do not meet the required score, you may be eligible to enroll in our presessional English language course.

Standard XII scores will not be considered for meeting our English Language requirements. Instead, applicants must complete an approved English Language test.

For Undergraduate programs:

- A minimum of 70% in Standard XII Higher Secondary School Certificate for CBSE, CISCE, Tamil Nadu, Maharashtra, and West Bengal boards.

- A minimum of 80% in Standard XII Higher Secondary School Certificate for other state boards.

For Postgraduate taught courses in ECE (Electronic and Computer Engineering):

- Bachelor's degree with a minimum CGPA of 6.5 out of 10 (equivalent to 2:2).

For Postgraduate taught courses in all other fields:

- Bachelor's degree with a minimum CGPA of 6.0 out of 10 (equivalent to 2:2).

Work experience may be required for certain courses. Specific course entry details can be found in the postgraduate prospectus.

Finding the Right Course

Every course is a unique blend of various elements, encompassing subjects covered, campus location, and potential career paths. Whether you are still considering different programs, weighing options between two fields of study, or unsure about your career aspirations, we are here to assist you in finding the most suitable course and coordinating your university application.

Start by jotting down a list of your interests and skills, and take some time to reflect on them. Identify the ones that show promise for pursuing as a career, and eliminate options that are merely hobbies. Creating a more focused and concise list of potential options will help you determine the best courses for your goals.

To make a well-informed decision and maximize your study abroad experience, utilize our course search feature to explore the available avenues tailored to your preferences.

Once you have narrowed your options, assess the qualifications required to pursue each path. Do you meet all the requirements? If not, consider whether you are willing to wait for another intake to fulfill the prerequisites or contemplate switching your area of focus. This decision may be challenging, but we are here to offer guidance and support.

Documents Required

You must submit certificates and diplomas from a recognized international higher education institution, verifying the completion of your degree(s). These documents must be officially issued by the Academic Registrar's Office, the Examinations Office, or the equivalent authority responsible for issuing official transcripts at your university.

It would be best if you also handed in transcripts of completed courses and grades for each semester within your degree. If you have transferred credits from previous studies, include official course transcripts. These transcripts should also be officially issued by the relevant office at your university.

Lastly, you need evidence that you meet the specific entry requirements for your chosen course or program. It is essential to refer to your university's website for information on the particular entry requirements and any additional documentation they may request, such as dissertations, essay summaries, letters of recommendation, or letters of intent. Only submit other documentation if explicitly requested by the university.

Citizenship / PR

A student visa is issued to those who plan to study in a recognized and approved academic institution in India. This visa applies to professional courses like Engineering, Medicine, Law, Management, etc., conducted by recognized educational institutions.

For school-level studies, a student visa is granted only to attend recognized international schools that admit international students and have higher fees.

Student visas are also available for music, dance, yoga, etc., but only in institutions recognized by the Ministry of Home Affairs, New Delhi.

Regarding permanent residency, there are different registration and naturalization options under the Citizenship Act 1955 for individuals of Indian origin, married to Indian citizens, or born to Indian parents. The Act also covers birth registration at Indian consulates and procedures for renouncing or resuming Indian citizenship.

Job Opportunities

The job market in India offers exciting opportunities in various high-paying fields. Professionals in Project Management hold a prominent position in ensuring successful project execution. Artificial Intelligence Engineers are crucial in advancing cutting-edge technology, while Data Scientists contribute significantly to data-driven decision-making.

Machine Learning Engineers are well-positioned to benefit from the growing AI landscape. Blockchain Developers are revolutionizing industries with secure and efficient solutions. Full Stack Software Developers remain in high demand, showcasing their software and website development versatility.

As India continues to embrace technological advancements, these top-paying careers promise a bright future for skilled and ambitious individuals.

Chapter 25

Ensuring Your Safety Abroad

Embarking on a journey to study abroad is a thrilling adventure filled with the promise of new experiences, cultures, and personal growth. However, with this excitement comes the need for careful preparation, especially when it comes to ensuring your health and safety. I will delve into the essential aspects of life abroad, offering comprehensive guidance on how to conduct yourself responsibly and confidently in unfamiliar territory. From securing your health and safety to familiarizing yourself with the legal landscape, I'll provide valuable insights and practical advice to help you maximize your study abroad experience while staying well-informed and respectful of your host country's customs and laws.

Safety

Prioritize your well-being with thorough pre-departure health preparations. Consult your healthcare provider for necessary vaccinations and prescriptions, and discuss any specific health concerns related to your travel plans. Secure comprehensive health insurance covering medical expenses, emergencies, and potential evacuation. Carry copies of essential documents (passport, visa, travel insurance) and store digital backups securely.

Research local healthcare resources (hospitals, clinics, pharmacies) and note emergency contact numbers for your destination. Prepare a health and safety kit with first aid, pain relievers, antiseptic wipes, and prescribed medications. Pack a small flashlight, pocketknife, and portable phone charger for unexpected situations. Stay informed about travel vaccinations and local health guidelines, including food and water safety.

Thoroughly understand your travel insurance policy's coverage and keep a physical copy and insurer contact information accessible. Embrace cultural awareness by researching local customs, laws, and regulations to ensure respectful interactions. Establish emergency contacts by sharing your itinerary and details with family or friends, and keep your embassy or consulate's contact information handy.

Traveling with others enhances safety, especially in unfamiliar areas or at night. Be aware of local emergency evacuation procedures and assembly points, particularly in your accommodation. Establish a communication plan with your study abroad program or university for emergencies. Stay informed about local news, especially in unstable regions or during natural disasters. Register with your embassy or consulate, if possible, for aid during emergencies. Trust your instincts: prioritize your safety and seek help if you feel uncomfortable or unsafe.

Healthcare System

First, research your host country's healthcare system to understand if it offers universal healthcare or requires private insurance.

For instance, Canada has a publicly funded system under the Canada Health Act. International students might be eligible for provincial/territorial coverage after a minimum six-month stay with a study permit (eligibility varies by region). Apply through your institution or directly with the provincial healthcare authority. While waiting for eligibility, private health insurance is necessary. Many institutions offer group plans, or you can purchase private insurance (e.g., Guard Me, Sun Life Financial). Costs and coverage differ by province, so understand your region's specifics.

In France, healthcare is universally funded by social security. International students aged 18-28 who have been studying for over three months may be eligible for French social security by applying at "La Sécurité Sociale Étudiante" upon arrival. Registration provides a "Carte Vitale" for accessing services. As social security doesn't cover everything, many students get complimentary "*mutuelle*" insurance (e.g., LMDE, MEP).

In the Netherlands, health insurance is mandatory for all residents, including international students, who must obtain Dutch health insurance (basic and supplementary coverage) even with home country insurance. Register with a provider using your Citizen Service Number (BSN), received upon arrival. Basic insurance costs around €100-€120 monthly; supplementary insurance (e.g., dental, physiotherapy) is extra.

Next, check specific health coverage requirements for international students in your host country, as many have mandatory enrollment in national systems, private insurance requirements, or a combination.

Identify your available options: enrolling in a national program (if eligible), purchasing private international student health insurance, or combining both for comprehensive coverage.

When considering private insurance, research and compare providers, noting coverage for medical services, prescriptions, and emergencies, as well as coverage limits, deductibles, and additional benefits (e.g., dental, vision).

The enrollment process varies by country and provider. You'll likely need to complete forms, provide proof of enrollment, and pay premiums. Understand the coverage start date, as it might be required immediately upon arrival.

Finally, maintain regular contact with your institution's international office for guidance on the local healthcare system and insurance requirements. They can also help with regulation changes or evolving needs during your stay.

Driver's License

Acquiring a driver's license in your host country can offer valuable mobility; however, the process varies significantly. Generally, it involves written exams, practical driving tests, and paperwork.

Typically, you'll begin by researching local requirements, including age restrictions and residency requirements. Once eligible, gather the necessary documents: proof of identity, residence, and a valid visa or permit.

After documentation, enrollment in a driving school or mandatory lessons may be required, varying in duration and content.

Most countries require passing a written theory exam on road rules, traffic signs, and safe driving. Study materials and practice exams are often available.

Passing the theory test usually leads to the practical driving test, where you demonstrate your driving skills to an examiner, assessing your ability to operate a vehicle safely and follow traffic rules. Practice is essential for this test.

In Germany, obtaining a Class B license (car) requires attending a certified driving school for theoretical and practical training. Applicants must be at least 17. After training, a theory and practical test are taken at the local driver's license authority (Fahrerlaubnisbehörde).

In India, the process can be complex due to varied state regulations. For a Class LMV license (car), you typically need to be 18, pass a written test on traffic rules, and then a practical driving test. Many states also have a learner's license stage before the full license.

In Italy, the Motorizzazione Civile issues licenses. For a Category B license (car), you must be at least 18, attend a driving school, pass a theory test, and take a practical driving test. International students also have specific requirements, including a residence certificate.

Remember that specific requirements and procedures can change, so always verify the most current information with local authorities or driving schools in your host country.

Local Laws

Familiarizing yourself with the local laws of your host country is crucial for a smooth and enjoyable study abroad experience. Understanding and adhering to these regulations helps you avoid legal issues and shows respect for the host country's culture and legal system. Begin by thoroughly researching local laws before your departure, covering traffic regulations, alcohol and drug laws, visa and immigration requirements, and cultural norms related to dress codes, public behavior, and social etiquette.

In Spain, traffic laws, including speed limits, parking regulations, and alcohol consumption limits while driving, are strictly enforced. Be aware of visa and immigration requirements, as overstaying can lead to severe consequences like deportation.

Ireland has strict alcohol consumption regulations, and public drunkenness can result in fines or arrests. The legal drinking age is 18, and responsible consumption is expected. Driving is on the left side of the road, a crucial rule to learn before driving.

In Japan, respecting local laws and customs is paramount. Etiquette and politeness are highly valued; for example, removing shoes before entering a home and bowing as a greeting are common. Japan has strict drug laws, with severe penalties, including imprisonment, for possessing even small amounts of illegal substances.

To ensure compliance, consult official government websites, embassy resources, or your host institution's international office for up-to-date information and guidance on your host country's legal and cultural norms.

Chapter 26

Immersing Yourself in the Host Culture

Immersing yourself in a foreign culture while studying abroad is profoundly rewarding, fostering understanding, connections, and personal and academic growth. Here are effective ways to fully embrace a new culture:

Learning the local language is key. Enroll in classes, practice with locals, and use language-learning tools. Proficiency enables authentic interactions and deeper cultural understanding.

Opt for homestays or shared housing with locals over international dorms. Living with residents provides firsthand exposure to daily life, customs, and traditions, offering language practice and lasting friendships.

Attend cultural events, festivals, and celebrations to gain unique insights into local traditions, music, dance, and cuisine. Participation offers a vibrant and memorable immersion.

Join university student clubs and organizations aligned with your interests (sports, arts, community service). These groups facilitate friendships and engagement in local activities with like-minded individuals.

Explore local cuisine by sampling dishes, trying street food, dining at local restaurants, and taking cooking classes to learn traditional meals. Food is an integral cultural aspect.

Travel within your host country to experience regional variations in customs, dialects, and traditions firsthand.

Enroll in classes or workshops teaching traditional skills or arts (dance, music, pottery, martial arts). Learning from local experts provides a deeper cultural connection.

Engage in volunteer work or community service projects to foster belonging and interact with locals while making a positive impact.

Explore the literature, films, and music of your host country for valuable insights into culture, history, and societal values.

Embrace cultural differences with an open mind and respect. Adapt to local customs and norms, even if they are different from your own. Respect facilitates meaningful connections and enriches your experience.

Document your journey and reflections through a journal, blog, or vlog. Sharing experiences helps process cultural immersion and provides a valuable record.

Remember that cultural immersion is gradual, with expected challenges. Be patient, embrace learning, and savor every moment of your cultural exploration.

Cultural Preparation

Cross-cultural preparation is essential for a successful study abroad experience. It equips you with the necessary knowledge, skills, and mindset to navigate and thrive in a foreign cultural context, enhancing safety, well-being, and respectful interaction with the host country's culture and people.

Adequate preparation helps you anticipate and manage culture shock, the disorientation from unfamiliar cultural norms. Understanding potential differences in communication styles, non-verbal cues, and social etiquette enables more effective communication and avoids misunderstandings.

Cross-cultural preparation fosters empathy and cultural sensitivity, promoting an appreciation for the host culture's values, customs, and traditions, leading to respectful interactions. It also enhances adaptability, a valuable skill during your time abroad and beyond.

For example, preparing for Japan involves understanding customs like bowing, gift-giving, and the importance of etiquette, as politeness and harmony are highly valued. Learning basic Japanese phrases can also be beneficial.

For India, preparation should encompass the country's diverse cultures, languages, and religions, recognizing regional variations in customs and traditions. Understanding the significance of festivals like Diwali and Holi and awareness of the caste system's social implications are essential for cultural sensitivity.

For Singapore, understanding its multicultural society with Chinese, Malay, Indian, and other ethnic groups is important. Familiarize yourself with their customs and traditions, such as Chinese New Year, Deepavali, and Hari Raya Puasa. Be aware of Singapore's strict laws on littering, public behavior, and drug offenses, as violations can result in severe penalties.

Consider cultural sensitivity training or workshops offered by universities or organizations. Engaging with individuals who have lived or studied in your host country can provide valuable insights. Maintaining an open, curious, and respectful attitude toward the host culture is key to positive interactions and a deeper appreciation of its richness.

Studying With Disabilities

Becoming part of a new culture as a student with disabilities requires preparation, adaptability, and a positive outlook. While unique challenges may arise, full cultural immersion and a meaningful experience are achievable.

Prior to your study abroad journey, research accessibility and available support in your host country. Learn about local disability rights laws, accessible transportation, and accommodations. Contact your host institution or program coordinators to discuss your specific needs and requirements. A well thought-out plan is key to navigating potential challenges effectively.

Many universities and programs offer disability support services, including accessible housing, academic accommodations, and assistance with daily tasks. Communicate your needs to program coordinators or the university's disability support office to ensure you receive the necessary services.

Research and connect with local disability organizations or support groups in your host country. They offer valuable insights into the local disability community, resources, and accessible activities. Engaging with these groups can also connect you with locals who share similar experiences.

Even if English is widely spoken, learning basic local phrases can greatly aid communication, show respect, and enhance interactions.

Participate in inaccessible cultural activities like local festivals, art exhibitions, or traditional performances (many offer accommodations like sign language interpreters or ramps). This allows cultural immersion and connection with locals.

Familiarize yourself with local transportation options and their accessibility features. Many cities have accessible public transport, and accessible taxis or rideshare services may be available, facilitating easier exploration.

Share your experiences and feedback with your host institution or program coordinators. Advocating for accessibility and inclusivity can improve support for future students with disabilities.

Build relationships with local students who share your interests or are involved in disability-related initiatives. These connections offer insights into daily life and provide a sense of belonging.

Embrace opportunities to step outside your comfort zone by trying local foods, engaging in cultural practices, and participating in traditions. These experiences can lead to meaningful connections and deeper cultural understanding.

Consider documenting your study abroad experience through a blog, vlog, or social media. Sharing your journey as a person with disabilities can inspire others, raise awareness, and provide a platform for information and resources.

Becoming part of a new culture as a student with disabilities may require extra planning, but it can be transformative and enriching. By seeking support, advocating for accessibility, and embracing cultural engagement, you can fully immerse yourself and create lasting memories.

Chapter 27

Making the Most of Your Time Abroad

Honing your cross-cultural skills while studying abroad enriches your experience and prepares you for a globalized world. Many universities offer cultural sensitivity training in their international programs, providing insights into cross-cultural communication, including nonverbal cues, customs, and etiquette.

1. **Language Learning:** Even basic phrases in the local language demonstrate respect and enable more meaningful interactions, significantly enhancing your cross-cultural skills.

2. **Interact with Locals:** Engage with residents by striking up conversations, attending local events, or participating in community activities. Building relationships offers invaluable cultural insights.

3. **Observe and Learn:** Pay attention to daily routines, traditions, and social norms. Notice greetings, dress, and polite behavior.

4. **Stay Open-Minded:** Embrace new experiences and perspectives. Avoid judgments based on your own cultural norms, try to understand the reasons behind different customs, and appreciate diverse beliefs.

For instance, in Spain, sharing tapas is common. Visiting local tapas bars and engaging with fellow diners allows you to experience this social aspect of dining. Participating in vibrant festivals and watching flamenco performances exposes you to Spanish culture and provides interaction with passionate locals.

In Dubai, cultural exchange centers like the Sheikh Mohammed Centre for Cultural Understanding (SMCCU) offer cultural meals, tours, and discussions with Emiratis, providing firsthand learning about their customs and values. During Ramadan, sharing iftar with Emirati friends offers an enlightening cultural experience.

In Russia, participating in Matryoshka doll painting workshops immerses you in Russian art and allows conversation with local artisans. Experiencing a Russian banya (sauna) with locals is a cultural adventure and social gathering.

Actively engaging in such cultural experiences and applying general cross-cultural tips enhances your ability to adapt and thrive in diverse cultural settings. Remember that cultural immersion is a journey requiring patience, an open heart, and a willingness to embrace the unfamiliar.

Learn From Your Mistakes

Learning from mistakes is crucial for personal, intellectual, and artistic growth while studying abroad and honing cultural skills. Errors are inevitable when navigating unfamiliar cultural terrain. Here's how to effectively learn from them:

Acknowledge Mistakes Openly: Recognize mistakes as natural and valuable for learning. Approach them with an open, growth-oriented mindset, avoiding shame or defensiveness.

Reflect on the Mistake: Take time to understand what went wrong and why. Consider the cultural context and any misinterpretations or assumptions that contributed to the error. Self-awareness is key.

Seek Feedback: Ask local friends, colleagues, or mentors for their perspectives. They can offer valuable insights on rectifying the mistakes and avoiding future ones. Constructive feedback is a valuable cultural learning resource.

Apologize and Make Amends: If your mistake caused offense, apologize sincerely. Demonstrating genuine remorse and a commitment to understanding and respecting the local culture can repair relationships.

Continue Learning: Treat each mistake as a learning opportunity. Study the cultural aspects involved, such as language, etiquette, or social norms. Consider cultural sensitivity workshops or language classes.

Challenge Assumptions: Be aware of your own cultural biases and preconceived notions. Actively seek to understand the perspectives and values of the host culture through conversations and attentive listening.

Embrace a Growth Mindset: Believe that your abilities can be developed through dedication and hard work. View mistakes as opportunities for improvement, not failures.

Stay Resilient: Don't let the fear of making mistakes prevent you from engaging in cultural experiences. Mistakes are part of the process, and resilience is vital for overcoming challenges and continuing your cultural learning.

Keep a Cultural Journal: Document your cultural experiences, including successes and mistakes. Writing helps with reflection and tracking progress.

Share Your Experiences: Share your cultural learning journey with others through blogs, social media, or conversations. Sharing can inspire others and reinforce your learning.

Remember that cultural competence is ongoing, and perfection is not the goal. Approaching mistakes as growth opportunities enhances your cultural skills and fosters a deeper understanding and appreciation of the host culture.

Plan Your Time

Planning your time abroad is crucial for a successful and enriching study experience. Effective planning helps you maximize opportunities, learn, and overcome challenges.

- **Academic Success:** Research and select courses aligning with your academic goals and degree requirements. Review schedules, prerequisites, and transfer policies to avoid setbacks.

- **Cultural Immersion:** Allocate time for local events, festivals, and activities to enhance your understanding of the host culture and interact with locals.

- **Language Learning:** If needed, plan for language courses and practice with locals to facilitate communication and deepen cultural understanding.

- **Travel Exploration:** Create a travel bucket list and budget to balance academic responsibilities with exploring nearby regions and countries.

- **Professional Development:** If possible, plan for internships or part-time work aligning with your field to gain practical experience and network.

- **Health and Well-being:** Research healthcare facilities, insurance, and health considerations. Ensure necessary vaccinations and medications are accessible.

- **Budget Management:** Develop a comprehensive budget that includes all expenses, factoring in currency exchange rates, and monitoring spending regularly.

- **Accommodation Arrangements:** Plan your housing (dorms, homestay, off-campus) in advance, ensuring safety and convenience.

- **Cultural Adaptation:** Study local customs, norms, and etiquette. Be open-minded, be patient, and seek support for cultural adjustment.

- **Emergency Preparedness:** Develop a contingency plan with emergency numbers, embassy contacts, and evacuation procedures. Keep important documents secure.

- **Time Management:** Create a weekly schedule balancing academics, cultural activities, and relaxation to maintain a healthy work-life balance.

- **Personal Goals:** Reflect on your objectives (self-confidence, worldview, independence) to guide your decisions and actions.

- **Stay Connected:** Maintain communication with family and friends for support and emotional well-being.

Effective planning allows you to make the most of this transformative experience, fostering personal and professional growth and creating lasting memories. While planning is key, remember to be flexible and open to unexpected opportunities and challenges.

Be A Part of Your Host Country's Cultural Milieu

Becoming an integral part of your host country's cultural milieu enriches your study abroad experience, deepening your understanding and fostering lasting connections. Consider these strategies:

Learn the Language: Dedicate time to learning the local language or basic phrases to enhance communication and participation in daily life.

Live with Locals: Opt for homestays or shared housing with locals to experience their daily routines, customs, and traditions firsthand.

Participate in Cultural Activities: Attend local cultural events, festivals, and celebrations for insights into traditional practices, music, dance, and cuisine.

Join Community Groups: Connect with locals who share your interests by joining community groups or clubs.

Explore Local Cuisine: Experiment with local dishes and street food, and dine at local restaurants as a delicious way to connect with the culture.

Travel Within the Country: Explore different regions within your host country, each with unique customs, dialects, and traditions.

Attend Local Classes or Workshops: Learn traditional skills or arts like dance, music, crafts, or cooking from local experts for a deeper cultural connection.

Volunteer: Contribute to the local community through volunteer work or service projects to foster belonging and interact with locals.

For example, in Australia, people can engage in outdoor activities like surfing or barbecues to connect with the local lifestyle. Respect Indigenous culture by attending events and visiting heritage sites.

In the Netherlands, embrace cycling to experience daily life and participate in national holidays like King's Day.

In Germany, attend festivals like Oktoberfest and Christmas markets to experience traditions and interact with locals. Learning German enhances cultural integration.

Approach cultural integration with an open mind, respect for local customs, and a willingness to adapt. Building relationships and actively participating in cultural activities will deepen your understanding and create lasting memories.

Work Opportunities

Exploring work opportunities in other countries can be an exciting and enriching experience, offering you a chance to gain international work experience, build your professional network, and immerse yourself in a different culture.

Internships: Interning abroad is a popular choice for students and recent graduates. It allows you to gain hands-on experience in your field of study, learn about international work practices, and enhance your resume. Many countries offer internships in various industries, including business, finance, technology, and hospitality.

Teaching English: Teaching English as a foreign language (TEFL) is a common way for native English speakers to work abroad. You can find opportunities to teach English in schools, language institutes, or private tutoring. This experience provides a source of income and allows you to engage with local communities and enhance your teaching skills.

Working Holiday Visas: Some countries, like Australia, New Zealand, Canada, and certain European nations, offer working holiday visas to young adults from eligible countries. These visas allow you to work and travel in the country for a specified period, typically one year. It's an excellent opportunity to fund your travels while gaining work experience.

Au Pair Programs: Au pair programs enable you to live with a host family in a foreign country and provide childcare in exchange for room, board, and a stipend. It's a cultural exchange opportunity that allows you to immerse yourself in a family's daily life and learn about their culture.

Research Positions: If you're pursuing graduate or postgraduate studies, consider research opportunities abroad. Collaborating with international research institutions or universities can broaden your academic horizons and contribute to your educational and career growth.

Freelancing and Remote Work: Many professionals can work from anywhere with the rise of remote work and the gig economy. Consider freelancing or remote work opportunities that allow you to work for international clients while residing in a foreign country.

Working for Multinational Companies: Some multinational companies hire employees to work in their overseas branches or offices. You may find job opportunities within these global organizations if you have specialized skills or qualifications.

Entrepreneurship: Launching a business or startup in a foreign country can be an entrepreneurial adventure. Research the local business environment, regulations, and market trends to determine if there are opportunities to start your venture.

Volunteer Work: While not typically paid, volunteer work abroad allows you to contribute to meaningful causes and gain valuable experience. Many volunteer programs provide room and board in exchange for your service.

Part-Time Jobs: Depending on the country's regulations and your visa status, you may be eligible for part-time work opportunities, such as working in restaurants, retail, or the service industry. Part-time jobs can help cover living expenses while abroad.

When exploring work opportunities in other countries, it's crucial to research visa requirements, work permits, and legal regulations. Additionally, consider your goals, skills, and interests to determine which work opportunity aligns best with your personal and professional aspirations.

Chapter 28

Seeking Immigration While Studying Abroad

Acquiring a Permanent Residency (PR) as an international student offers significant benefits and opportunities. Many host countries provide pathways for students to obtain PR status.

Pathways to PR for Students Abroad

Post-study work visas in countries like Canada, Australia, and the UK allow graduates to gain work experience, a stepping stone to PR.

Skilled migration programs assess applicants based on factors like age, education, work experience, and language proficiency, offering another route to PR.

Family sponsorship can be an option if the student has family members who are PR holders or citizens in the host country.

Provincial Nominee Programs (PNPs) in some countries, like Canada, allow provinces to nominate students for PR based on their economic needs.

Entrepreneurial and investor programs, such as the US EB-5 visa, offer PR for individuals who invest in job-creating businesses or start businesses.

Benefits of PR While Studying Abroad

PR provides a long-term stay, fostering stability and deeper cultural immersion.

It offers enhanced work flexibility and expanded job opportunities without the restrictions of student visas.

Access to government-funded healthcare and education, often with reduced tuition fees, alleviates financial burdens.

PR can be a step towards citizenship, granting the same rights as native-born citizens, including voting.

It eliminates the need for visa renewals, simplifying administrative processes.

Social benefits like unemployment benefits and pension plans are typically available to PR holders, providing a safety net.

PR simplifies international travel by allowing easier re-entry to the host country.

Family reunification is often easier with PR, allowing sponsorship of family members.

Note that acquiring PR typically involves a multi-step process with specific criteria. Consulting an immigration expert or your institution's international office is advisable.

Benefits of Relocating Abroad

Relocating to another country presents a transformative experience, yielding numerous benefits encompassing personal growth, cultural enrichment, and professional advancement. This life-changing decision, whether driven by educational pursuits, career aspirations, or a desire for a new lifestyle, offers advantages that can profoundly shape an individual's perspective and capabilities.

One of the most significant aspects of relocating abroad is the opportunity for substantial personal growth and self-discovery. Navigating a new environment necessitates adaptation, fostering valuable skills such as resilience, problem-solving abilities, and independence. Exposure to diverse cultures, customs, and ways of thinking broadens one's perspective and cultivates enhanced global awareness. This intercultural competence proves to be an invaluable asset in an increasingly interconnected world, enriching both personal and professional spheres.

Cultural immersion stands out as another compelling advantage of living in a foreign country. This direct engagement with a culture in its authentic context allows for meaningful interactions with locals, active participation in cultural activities, and the potential acquisition of a new language. Such deep cultural understanding cultivates empathy and tolerance, fostering a more open-minded and accepting approach to diverse perspectives, thereby enriching one's life in profound and meaningful ways.

Professionally, relocating to another country can significantly enhance career prospects by providing opportunities to gain international work experience, a highly valued attribute in today's global job market. Building a diverse professional network and acquiring unique skills can set individuals apart from their peers. Employers increasingly recognize the value of candidates with international experience, appreciating their adaptability, cross-cultural communication skills, and capacity to navigate diverse work environments effectively.

Furthermore, moving abroad can unlock access to unique educational opportunities, including prestigious universities, specialized programs, and advanced research facilities that align with specific academic and career goals. This chance to receive a potentially transformative education can provide a significant competitive edge in one's chosen field.

From a lifestyle perspective, relocating often introduces individuals to an improved quality of life. Many countries offer superior healthcare systems, enhanced safety, and comprehensive social services, all contributing to increased well-being. The exploration of different cuisines, diverse landscapes, and varied recreational activities can be an exhilarating and enriching experience, fostering lasting memories and a deeper appreciation for the world's inherent diversity.

While the transition to a new country may present challenges, such as navigating bureaucratic processes, adapting to a new language, and experiencing homesickness, these difficulties ultimately contribute to personal resilience and growth. Overcoming these obstacles fosters a sense of accomplishment and develops valuable life skills that extend far beyond the experience of studying abroad.

How to Acquire Permanent Residence

Obtaining Permanent Residency (PR) varies significantly across countries, each with its own distinct rules and eligibility criteria.

Navigating these systems often requires careful attention to specific requirements and procedures.

In **Canada**, the Express Entry system, a points-based system evaluating factors like age, education, work experience, and language proficiency, is a popular route to PR. Completing a Canadian post-secondary program can enhance a candidate's points, making it advantageous for international students.

Australia employs a similar points-based system called the General Skilled Migration (GSM) program. After submitting an Expression of Interest (EOI) and receiving an invitation, candidates can apply for a skilled visa. International students can transition to the Temporary Graduate Visa (Subclass 485) post-studies, which can lead to PR through skilled migration.

The United States typically grants PR based on employment or family sponsorship. Employment-based categories like EB-2 and EB-3 require employer sponsorship. Some students may transition from Optional Practical Training (OPT) or the H-1B visa to employment-based PR. Family-based PR is an option for relatives of U.S. citizens or permanent residents.

The United Kingdom offers routes to PR, such as the Tier 2 (General) work visa, leading to Indefinite Leave to Remain (ILR) after five years of continuous residence following employment after studies. Ancestry visas, for those with a UK-born grandparent, can also lead to ILR.

New Zealand utilizes a points-based system for PR through the Skilled Migrant Category (SMC), assessing health, character, age, work experience, and qualifications. Completing a recognized New Zealand qualification can earn international students additional points.

The European Union (EU) has diverse immigration programs across its member states. For instance, in Germany, graduates with a job offer may qualify for the EU Blue Card, a pathway to PR. Other EU countries offer options like investment-based visas, family reunification, or long-term residency permits.

China's PR policies often hinge on employment and family ties. Foreigners working and residing in China for a specified period and paying taxes may be eligible. Family members of Chinese citizens or PR holders can also apply.

The United Arab Emirates (UAE) provides several pathways to PR, including investment-based visas, skilled worker visas, and long-term residency permits, catering to entrepreneurs, professionals, and retirees.

Given the complexity and uniqueness of each country's immigration system, consulting with immigration experts, legal professionals, or the respective country's immigration authorities is crucial for understanding the specific requirements and procedures for acquiring PR in your chosen destination.

Chapter 29

Studying Abroad Experience for Global Growth in Country of Birth

Building Your Skills

Building on the experiences and skills acquired during your study abroad journey is crucial for maximizing the benefits of this transformative period. Begin by reflecting on the significant personal and professional lessons learned, identifying acquired skills, challenges overcome, and areas of personal growth. This self-assessment will illuminate your strengths and areas for development.

Maintain the cultural sensitivity and awareness cultivated abroad by remaining open to diverse perspectives in your home country. Seek opportunities to engage with people from various backgrounds through cultural events, volunteering, or multicultural groups. If you improve your language skills, continue to utilize them by joining language clubs, finding exchange partners, or tutoring others, recognizing their value in personal and professional contexts.

Nurture the relationships established abroad, staying in touch with international friends and contacts for insights, networking opportunities, and potential collaborations. Seek out international activities and events in your home country, such as cultural festivals or conferences, to maintain a connection with your global experiences.

If you developed an interest in international affairs, consider pursuing a related career in fields like diplomacy, international business, or global development, where your study abroad experience can be a significant asset. Explore further education with a postgraduate degree in international studies or a subject ignited by your time abroad to gain specialized knowledge and enhance career prospects.

Participate in global organizations like international chambers of commerce or cultural associations to engage with like-minded individuals and collaborate on global initiatives. Seek mentorship from those who have successfully leveraged their study abroad experiences for guidance in translating your experiences into meaningful career paths.

Utilize your new skills and perspectives to contribute to your community through volunteering, sharing your experiences with local schools, or participating in development projects. Commit to lifelong learning by continuously exploring new cultures, languages, and perspectives through various means.

The skills and experiences gained during your study abroad journey are valuable assets that will continue to shape your life and career long after your return.

Global Growth In Your Home Country

Bringing global growth to your home country is an impactful endeavor that leverages the knowledge and skills gained during your study abroad experience to contribute to national development and cross-cultural understanding.

International business and trade offer primary avenues for this. Utilize your international connections to establish partnerships, export products, or expand markets, stimulating economic growth and creating job opportunities. Promoting cultural exchange through collaborations with educational institutions facilitates student exchange programs and intercultural workshops, equipping future generations with global perspectives.

If you developed an entrepreneurial spirit, consider launching a startup that leverages international insights to address local or global challenges, fostering economic growth and innovation. Forge international partnerships in research, education, and technology to drive economic and intellectual growth through shared resources and knowledge transfer.

Promote cultural exchange and appreciation by organizing festivals and events that celebrate global diversity, enrich society, and create economic opportunities for local artists. Engage in diplomacy and advocacy for policies that encourage international cooperation and sustainable development.

If you're passionate about philanthropy, establish or contribute to initiatives addressing global challenges in healthcare, education, or environmental conservation. Share your experiences and knowledge with those interested in international careers, empowering future global leaders.

Collaborate with research institutions on international research and innovation projects, contributing to global growth in technology, health, and sustainability. Engage in public awareness campaigns to increase understanding of international affairs and global challenges, fostering a global mindset.

Your study abroad journey positions you as a catalyst for change. By actively engaging in these initiatives, you can contribute to your home country's development and a more interconnected world.

Chapter 30

Wrapping It All Up!

This book has served as your guide to the expansive world of international education, illuminating the transformative power of studying abroad. We've explored the multifaceted journey of relocating to a new country, immersing yourself in diverse cultures, accessing quality education, and forging connections with people from around the globe.

We've also highlighted how this experience can significantly boost your career prospects and foster profound personal growth, regardless of your educational stage. From secondary school to postgraduate studies, we've shown how studying abroad cultivates new skills, expands your professional network, and exposes you to varied and enriching teaching methodologies.

Furthermore, we've provided insights into navigating the financial aspects of this adventure. Our aim has been to demystify the complexities of international education, equipping you with the essential knowledge and inspiration to confidently take the life-changing step of studying abroad – a journey poised to simplify, enrich, and fundamentally transform your life.

Here's a concise recap of the key areas we've covered:

Moving Abroad and Making Your Life Easier: Relocating internationally is a significant decision brimming with opportunities for a transformative experience that can simplify your life in unforeseen ways. This transition necessitates considering migration processes, the multifaceted benefits of studying abroad, the enriching exposure it provides, the access to quality education, the introduction to new cultures and people, the resulting career prospects, and the immense personal growth it fosters.

How Can One Migrate Abroad?: International migration is a complex undertaking demanding meticulous planning and execution. It involves securing necessary visas, permits, and documentation, understanding intricate immigration laws, and potentially navigating language and cultural differences. Exploring various visa options, such as work visas, student visas, and skilled worker programs, is crucial and depends on individual goals. Thorough research, careful preparation, and potentially seeking guidance from immigration experts or agencies can streamline this process and enhance the likelihood of a successful migration.

Benefits of Studying Abroad: The advantages of studying abroad are extensive. Beyond academic achievements, it provides deep immersion in a new culture, cultivating cultural sensitivity and a broader global perspective. Exposure to diverse teaching styles and learning environments sharpens critical thinking skills and enhances adaptability. This experience often leads to enduring friendships, an expanded personal and professional network, and significant personal growth, all of which are invaluable for both personal and career development.

The Exposure That Comes: A primary benefit of studying abroad is the profound exposure it offers. Living in a foreign country introduces you to novel traditions, customs, and an entirely different way of life. This cultural immersion fosters open-mindedness, a deeper comprehension of global issues, and the capacity to appreciate and respect a wide range of perspectives.

Quality Education

Quality education is a cornerstone of studying abroad. Many renowned universities and institutions worldwide offer world-class education, and this exposure can significantly impact your academic and professional future. It allows you to gain access to top-notch faculty, research opportunities, and state-of-the-art facilities that can shape your knowledge and skills for years to come.

New Culture, New People

Moving abroad is not just about academics but also about embracing a new culture and connecting with new people. Interacting with individuals from different backgrounds enriches your life in countless ways. It broadens your horizons and helps you develop a global mindset. The friendships formed during this time can be lasting and may open doors to exciting opportunities and experiences.

Career Opportunities

Studying abroad can significantly enhance your career prospects. Employers often value candidates with international exposure, as they tend to possess a broader skill set, adaptability, and a deeper understanding of global markets. It also provides access to internships, co-op programs, and networking opportunities that can jumpstart your career.

Personal Growth

Personal growth is an inherent part of studying abroad. Living in a foreign country forces you to step out of your comfort zone, face new challenges, and develop self-reliance and resilience. This personal growth can positively affect your self-confidence, problem-solving abilities, and overall life skills.

Benefits of Studying Abroad for School Students

For school students, studying abroad can be an enriching experience that goes beyond the classroom. It encourages independence and self-sufficiency from a young age. School students have the opportunity to engage with diverse cultures and gain a global perspective that can shape their future academic and career choices.

Benefits of Studying Abroad for Undergraduate Students

Undergraduate students can benefit immensely from studying abroad. Beyond acquiring academic qualifications, they can learn new skills in and out of the classroom. This period is ideal for personal growth, self-discovery, and building a global network that can provide lifelong support.

How Graduate-Level Students Can Benefit from Studying Abroad

Graduate-level students can take advantage of the advanced education and specialized knowledge available abroad. They gain exposure to different teaching styles, research opportunities, and the potential for a great career. Additionally, graduate-level studies can boost their confidence, encouraging independent thinking and research skills.

How To Choose the Right Program for You

Selecting the right program is essential for a successful overseas education experience. Key factors to consider are your academic and career goals, personal interests, and preferred destination. Additionally, evaluate the type of program (e.g., exchange, degree, or language course) that best suits your needs and budget, as well as the program's duration and cultural fit.

How to Find the Right Kind of Funding Sources

Financing your education abroad can be challenging, but numerous funding sources are available. These sources include scholarships, grants, part-time work opportunities, and student loans. Finding the proper funding that matches your financial situation and educational needs is crucial to making your dream of studying abroad a reality.

Study Abroad Checklist for the USA

This chapter provides a comprehensive checklist for students aspiring to study in the United States. It includes information on visa requirements, university selection, financial planning, standardized tests, application processes, and considerations for cultural adjustment. The USA is one of the top destinations for international students, and this chapter offers vital guidance to ensure a smooth transition and successful academic journey.

Study Abroad Checklist for Canada

For those considering Canada as their study destination, this chapter outlines the necessary steps for a successful experience. It covers visa applications, choosing the right Canadian institution, financial preparation, English proficiency requirements, and other practical advice. Canada is known for its diverse and inclusive education system, and this checklist will help prospective students make the most of their time in the country.

Study Abroad Checklist for the UK

Studying in the United Kingdom is a dream for many international students. This chapter offers insights into the UK's educational landscape, visa processes, university selections, scholarships, and considerations for adapting to the British culture. It's a valuable resource for those looking to embark on their academic journey in the UK.

Study Abroad Checklist for Australia

Australia is renowned for its high-quality education and vibrant lifestyle. In this chapter, students will find guidance on student visa applications, selecting the right Australian institution, financial planning, English language requirements, and tips for embracing the Australian way of life. The checklist equips aspiring students with valuable information to make their experience in Australia a success.

Study Abroad Checklist for Singapore

Singapore is an emerging hub for international education, and this chapter delves into the intricacies of studying in this dynamic city-state. It covers student pass applications, university choices, financial considerations, and cultural tips to adapt to Singapore's cosmopolitan environment. The checklist aids students in preparing for a unique educational journey in Singapore.

Study Abroad Checklist for Dubai

The United Arab Emirates, particularly Dubai, has become a prominent destination for international students. This chapter offers valuable insights into visa requirements, university options, financial planning, and adjusting to life in the UAE. As Dubai grows as an education hub, this checklist is a valuable tool for students considering this location.

Study Abroad Checklist for Denmark

Denmark is known for its high-quality education and quality of life. This chapter outlines visa procedures, choosing Danish institutions, financial aspects, and tips for cultural integration. It provides an essential guide for students exploring the Scandinavian education system.

Study Abroad Checklist for the Netherlands

The Netherlands is a popular destination for international students, and this chapter offers guidance on Dutch student visas, university choices, financial planning, and tips for embracing the Dutch culture. It serves as a roadmap for students considering the vibrant academic landscape of the Netherlands.

Study Abroad Checklist for Sweden

Sweden's education system is known for its innovation and quality. This chapter explores the steps to study in Sweden, including visa applications, university selections, financial aspects, and adapting to Swedish life and culture. It's an invaluable resource for those considering higher education in Sweden.

Study Abroad Checklist for Switzerland

Switzerland is synonymous with excellence in education. This chapter offers insights into Swiss student visas, university choices, financial planning, and recommendations for thriving in the Swiss academic environment. Aspiring students can rely on this checklist for a successful study abroad experience in Switzerland.

The chapters in the book provide in-depth checklists and guidance for studying in other countries, including Russia, India, Germany, Italy, Spain, France, Hungary, China, Ireland, New Zealand, and Japan. Additionally, the book addresses crucial topics like ensuring your safety abroad, immersing yourself in the host culture, making the most of your time abroad, and seeking immigration opportunities while studying abroad. Each chapter is a valuable resource for students planning to pursue their education in these respective countries, offering a holistic view of the considerations and steps needed for a successful international academic experience.

You can schedule a consultation call with our experts if you have further inquiries.

We help you move abroad by giving you the necessary advice and information. Trust us to guide you every step of the way!

We know much about immigration laws and can give you personalized advice on moving abroad. We'll help you find the best way to move to your dream country.

Want to learn more?

Contact: Discovery Call with Ashwin Patel

Or drop us an email at ashwin@moveabroad.co